MY WORLD
WAS TOO SMALL

MY WORLD WAS TOO SMALL

by Ruth Peterman

TYNDALE
HOUSE
PUBLISHERS Inc.
Wheaton, Illinois

COVERDALE HOUSE
PUBLISHERS Ltd.
London, England

Library of Congress Cata-
log Card Number 74-
79608. ISBN 8423-4658-
9. Copyright © 1974
by Tyndale House Pub-
lishers, Wheaton, Illi-
nois. All rights reserved.
First printing, June 1974.
Printed in United States
of America.

To Clint

Contents

Acknowledgments

Several chapters of *My World Was Too Small* appeared originally in periodicals. Tyndale House gratefully acknowledges permission to adapt and reprint these articles:

"Test of Faith" is reprinted by permission from *Lutheran Women* (official publication of Lutheran Church Women, Lutheran Church in America) November 1973, page 31.

"Fathers Who Pray," copyright © 1971, and "Why, God?" copyright © 1964, are reprinted from *Sunday Digest* and are used by permission of David C. Cook Publishing Co., Elgin, Illinois.

"Tents and Toes," "Celebration," "Saved from Death," "Is There Any Comfort for Parents?" "My Long-haired Son," and "Breakfast Guest" are all reprinted from *Scope,* official journal of the American Lutheran Church Women, where they appeared under the copyright of Augsburg Publishing House.

"Demonstration" is reprinted by permission of *The Lutheran Standard.*

"What I Learned from Bell's Palsy" is reprinted from *Church Administration,* August 1967. Copyright © 1967 The Sunday School Board of the Southern Baptist Convention. All rights reserved. Used by permission.

"The Day Doubt Disappeared" and "If the Smiths Hadn't Gone to Texas" are reprinted from *Light and Life Evangel,* by permission of Light and Life Press, Winona Lake, Indiana.

"Requiem" is reprinted by permission of *War Cry,* official publication of the Salvation Army.

The Governor

After working for several years as a precinct chairwoman for my political party, I was asked to head our ward for our state gubernatorial candidate. I worked very hard and when he won, I received an invitation to the inaugural ball. That Christmas I got a card from him showing him with his family. On the outside of the card was a picture of the mansion. A few months later, I got an autographed ten-by-fourteen colored picture of him. My children were even more impressed than I was, and that picture went to school for show-and-tell.

Two years later, when we went to the state convention, I was with the ward chairwoman, greeting friends and waiting for important convention business to start. We met the governor coming down the hall with another prominent official. My friend stopped, put out her hand, and said, "Hello, Harold." To my intense surprise, he replied, "Hello, Marie. Good to see you."

That day I saw the difference between knowing a person and being known by him. I had worked hard for that governor. I'd have recognized him any place on the earth. But he didn't know me. He was introduced to me that afternoon for the first time. In spite of his invitation, his Christmas card, and autographed portrait, I was unknown to him.

People often ask, "Do you know God?" I tell them I do; I've known him all my life. My parents introduced me to Jesus when I was so young that it seems there was never a day I didn't know him.

But do you know what's even better?

He knows me.

I am the Good Shepherd and know my sheep and they know me. John 10:14, TLB

But if any man love God, the same is known of him.
1 Corinthians 8:3

Father, to be known by one so great as you is more than we can comprehend. Help us to remember that you know every one of us by name. Amen.

Fathers Who Pray

We hear of unbelievably dramatic escapes from death and of sudden conversions as a result of a "mother's prayers." Hymn-writers, too, seem to indicate more praying mothers than fathers.

I sat in one group held in unbearable suspense as the speaker told all that went wrong with an airplane he was in during the worst possible weather. He got through safely. Later he learned that his mother had been praying for him that night.

One person tells of recovery from drug addiction. Another tells of conversion after a life of alcoholism. A rebellious teen-ager accepts Christ. All three credit their mother's prayers for their changed lives.

Don't people have praying fathers? I did. And so do my children.

The Bible's warnings for spiritual concern over the children is more frequently addressed to fathers than to mothers. God says over and over in the books of the law, "ye fathers. . . ." Job made offerings to God lest his children had sinned when they were out partying. Today's kids should know when they're out on the town that their dad, as well as Mother, is concerned and praying they'll do right.

I have no doubt that my father's prayers matched my mother's in fervency. In the earliest years of my childhood, perhaps because of mother's ill health, it was my father who taught me my prayers and told me Bible stories. He listened to my "golden text" for Sunday school and to my "Bible text" for catechism. Every day he led the family in prayer.

I lived at home longer than my brothers and sister did, because my husband was overseas during World War II. During those years, I daily heard both my parents pray for their children gone from home. While they had good reason to plead for the physical safety of my oldest brother, as the war had taken him to Guadalcanal, their prayers more often showed concern for his spiritual needs. They weren't naive about the temptations besetting us.

In their own way, they (like Job) made sacrifices on behalf of their children. At times when I thought my parents were in bed I would approach their bedside to say goodnight, and often, my father was still on his knees by the bed.

It has been twenty-eight years since I left that shelter. Until he died, my father, as well as my mother, wrote me every week, telling the news, discussing ideas, and assuring me of their prayers.

My husband is no less concerned about our children than my father was about us. Daily, they see him pray. Like my father, my husband is the spiritual leader in our home. He makes a sacrifice (of prayer) each night upon retiring, but then, like the psalmist, he "both lays him down and sleeps." I, on the other hand, tend to stay awake, as though God needed my alertness to bring the children safely through the night. Could it be that children grow up more aware of their mother's prayers, not because their mothers have greater faith than their fathers, but rather because their mothers are lighter sleepers?

Yes, the Bible emphasizes fathers. While not everyone has a father like mine, or like my children have, I believe there are more praying fathers than we realize. Together — one in mind and fervency, in training, example, and prayer — my parents, with the Holy Spirit, established my feet on that heavenward path.

My mother's *and my father's* prayers have followed me.

Young men, listen to me as you would to your father. Listen and grow wise, for I speak the truth — don't turn away. For I, too, was once a son, tenderly loved by my mother as an only child, and the companion of my father. He told me never to forget his words. "If you follow them," he said, "you will have a long and happy life." Proverbs 4:1-4

Father, thank you for fathers who so instruct and live before their children that they know they'll never get away from their fathers' prayers. Amen.

You Never Know

 When you do something to help a stranger, you never know how far you may travel with that person before a door closes between you.

On my way out of church one Sunday, I saw an old fellow struggling into his coat. I lifted the dirty, threadbare sleeve so he could get his arm into it. He thanked me with radiant face.

A week later, I saw him again. He recognized me and we shook hands. I told him my name. "Have you gone here long?"

"No. A few months. My name's Gus. Gus Johnson."

"Do you live near here?"

"On the other side of the park. I walk."

I offered him a ride and for two years we drove Gus home from church every Sunday.

Gradually we learned a little about him. He'd been an alcoholic for many years until some of the men of our church who conducted street meetings pointed him to a better life. He spoke of "before" and "after" the day he'd put his faith in Christ, as if that day was a meridian in his life.

Gus's ruddy face appears before my mind as clearly today as it did each Sunday that he rode with us. His large, very blue eyes beamed kindliness and good will.

We never brought Gus home with us for dinner. I've since often wondered why. We frequently had guests, relatives and friends. It would have been so easy to include him.

One Sunday, Gus wasn't in church. The following week, when he was still absent, we went to his room. He showed us a large growth on his abdomen. He said he was going to City Hospital the next day. I've since wondered how he got there. We took him a hot meal that night and promised to visit him in the hospital.

Gus never told us what disease he had. After his surgery, he had a sudden setback and needed blood, which my husband was able to give.

One night, the telephone rang. It was the nurse on Gus's station. "Gus Johnson is very sick. It's doubtful he'll make it through the night. Would you like to see him?"

"I certainly would. Have his relatives been called?"

"He has no one. You're the only one he gave in case of emergency."

I hung up the phone. Was Gus really that alone? Why hadn't I guessed it? Why hadn't we invited him to come to dinner sometimes and spend Christmas with us? Alone. Dying.

We hurried to the hospital. While my husband parked the car, I went at once to Gus. I bent over him. His breath came hard. His face seemed hot and his enormous eyes glistened. I had never seen a dying person before. Eternity seemed to be pressing in upon us.

"Gus," I said, "Gus, can you hear me?"

There was no answer except a change in the expression of his eyes. I continued, "Are you going to see Jesus tonight?" It seemed that glory transformed his face.

I thought, "This man is only moments from standing in the presence of God."

"Gus," I whispered, "when you see Jesus, will you give him my love?" His eyes showed he understood.

Bearing my message, Gus passed into eternity.

When you put out a hand to help a stranger you never know how far you may go with him.

She stretcheth out her hand to the poor; yea, she reacheth forth her hands to the needy.

Proverbs 31:20

Father, I could have done so much more for Gus. Help me to see all the Guses around me and to ease their loneliness by sharing the happiness and home you've entrusted to me and my family. Amen.

Habakkuk Here and Now

For my devotions, I'd read the last portion of Habakkuk, which was Habakkuk's prayer. It had stirred me and I'd felt blessed by it, but it hadn't really spoken to my problems. I didn't have any fig trees that might fail to blossom or any vines that might fail to bear grapes. I had no olive trees to worry about, and no fields, no sheep, no cows. This obviously was addressed to an agrarian people.

What I did have was a dry spell in my writing. My manuscripts were all coming back and I wondered if ever again I'd have an idea that would sell. I also had worries about my children. They didn't all show the devotion to God that I prayed they would. I had a dull headache as a result of one more night spent wrestling with the noise of barking dogs. I wished Habakkuk had said something about that.

Then I picked up the Bible again and reread the third chapter. When I got to the 17th and 18th verses, I read them several times. It seemed that Habakkuk was speaking to my problems after all. Changing it slightly, and with compliments to Habakkuk for being a better poet, I paraphrased it this way:

"Though the idea will not blossom, neither shall a check be in the mail; my labor as a mother seem wasted, and the children appear worldly; though sleep be slow in coming and dogs bark louder each night: Yet I will rejoice in the Lord, I will joy in the God of my salvation."

For the rest of the day, I had fun paraphrasing that passage to fit my needs. Then I started wondering if it could be made to fit those of every age and circumstance. For the old, I substituted: "Though the body age and grow weary, neither shall the social security check be on time; though the children seldom come and see me, and their letters are few and far between; though this old home be depressing, and I feel neglected and unloved: Yet. . . ."

I thought of my husband's problems and read it this way:

"Though work at the office be endless, neither shall good help be possible to find; though the bid for that job shall fail, and inflation consume all my pay; though my wife be depressed, and my stomach in knots: Yet. . . ."

I paraphrased it for younger people too:

"Though the labor market be flooded, and there be no job for me; the cramming for tests shall fail, and the course shall yield no credit; though the girl I want won't have me, and my folks think I'm a hippie: Yet. . . ."

To finish my devotions that day, I turned to Philippians 4. "Rejoice in the Lord alway and again I say rejoice."

Could any circumstance of life keep me from saying,

8

"Yet will I rejoice in the Lord, I will joy in the God of my salvation"?

Father, thank you that the one certainty we have in life is your constant love. Today I will joy in the God of my salvation. Amen.

Test of Faith

 David was born in November 1959. We brought him home to our four children and felt we were the happiest family in all Minneapolis. What a Thanksgiving we had that year!

But David had colic. Starting at around two weeks, he fussed day and night. When he was six weeks old, he seemed to have the flu. We gave him the peppermint-smelling medicine the doctor had prescribed, but he could hold nothing in his stomach. He would eat hungrily, then vomit suddenly and lose it all. He became noticeably thinner. When I became fearful that he had more than a simple flu, I consulted "Dr. Spock" and found David's symptoms accurately described.

We took him back to the doctor.

"I think there's an obstruction that prevents passage of his food, doctor," I said. He said he was beginning to think the same thing. We had prayed that a correct diagnosis might be made so proper treatment might begin at once. While the doctor was examining David's abdomen, he suddenly said excitedly, "Here it is. It came right under my fingers."

A gristle-like band was preventing passage of food from the pylorus into the duodenum. The condition is called pyloric stenosis. The stomach contracts whenever it tries to force food through the pylorus. It was this contraction that caused David's "projectile vomiting," I learned. A contraction had also brought the gristle-like band under the doctor's fingers so that he could make a proper diagnosis.

Surgery would be relatively simple; they wouldn't have to cut into any organs of the body, but merely snip off that gristle-like band.

We took David to the hospital that night. The doctor ordered intravenous feedings. For a week, he had retained no food and had grown very thin. Any sudden or loud noise such as a sneeze or cough would cause him to burst into a high, weak, pitiable cry.

They took David into another room for a few minutes. Then they brought him back, screaming and wild-eyed, to his bed. I learned they had cut an opening near his ankle where the intravenous tube was slipped into his little vein. "He's ready if he should need a blood transfusion tomorrow, too," the doctor explained. This had been done without anesthesia.

Our seven-weeks-old baby looked at me with enormous, panic-stricken eyes. He screamed, pleading to be picked up, something I couldn't do on account of the feeding apparatus. He screamed at a high pitch as long as we were there. My husband finally led me away; it was more than either of us could stand.

We went home. That was one of the saddest nights of my life. I felt this night would really test my faith. I wrestled with the possibility of losing my baby. My 13-year-old daughter was angry at God. "If he takes David away from us, after letting us have him for seven weeks, I'll never forgive him!"

Sleep eluded me. I continued to hear my baby scream and see his terrified eyes. I knew God knew best and that he loved me. I knew that in his love for me he could take my baby out of my arms and to himself. But how I wanted to keep my baby.

Morning came. I had given David up, should God choose to take him. In my heart I felt he was going to.

When we returned to the hospital, David's little thin face had grown puffy from more water in his tissues than he had ever had before. He looked fat. Two friends came to be with us. We talked lightly as we waited for the hour of surgery. But when a nurse came in, picked up David, and carried him out of the room, our composure wilted. I went into my husband's arms and wept.

God spared David. His weak little body came through without complications. The following day he drank water from a bottle and four hours after that, I nursed him again.

My faith had been tested. God had asked me, "Do you really believe that I know what's best for you and your family?" In my deepest distress, I had felt no bitterness against God — only sadness at what I had feared he might do.

Now my task remained: to instill in our children the faith that believes, "You know best."

Christian Reflexes

Joe Frazier, one-time boxing champion, refers to preparation, whether for boxing or for life, as "roadwork." "You got to do your own roadwork. Everybody's got some kind of roadwork, whether you're settin' out to be a secretary, lawyer, nurse, or salesman. If you don't have that roadwork done, nobody can help you."

Joe says, "You can map out a fight plan or a life plan. But when the action starts, it may not go the way you planned, and you're down to your reflexes — which means your training. That's where your roadwork shows. If you cheated on that in the dark of the mornin', well, you're gettin' found out now under the bright lights."[1]

What a sermon! Taken spiritually, what constitutes "roadwork" for a Christian who wants to stay on his feet through the thick of the "fight"? In boxing, it's practice and discipline. Joe Frazier disciplines his body, putting it through strenuous training starting in the "dark of the mornin'."

What do we do to keep fit spiritually? Do we search the Scriptures? I mean really search them, comparing Scripture with Scripture? Joe's training doesn't consist of reading a small "inspirational" in the morning about some fighter who made it. Joe has to work to train himself. How about our prayer life? Daniel prayed three times a day. In the New Testament, Paul says we should pray without ceasing. I understand this to mean that we live in such a spirit of communion with God

---

[1]Excerpt from "The Champ, Joe Frazier!" by William D. Ellis. The Reader's Digest, January 1972. Copyright 1971 by The Reader's Digest Assn., Inc.

that we pray as we breathe. This comes with practice and soul discipline.

What about divine worship? "I didn't make it to church this morning." How often have you heard that? I don't make it to church either unless I get out of bed at a proper time and just plain go. Clocks that get people to work five days a week seem inoperative on Sundays.

I suppose it's possible that one could read the Bible diligently, pray faithfully, never miss church, and still be unprepared for the hardships that come. How can I know that if someone dearest on earth to me were suddenly snatched away in death I would remain strong in my faith? Until tragedy strikes you, you wonder about this. God's Word assures us that he will never leave us or forsake us.

But how can we prepare for tragedy? I think it's through day-by-day obedience to what you believe is God's purpose for your life. This means not only to go when he says "Go," but to learn to stop when he says "Stop." Someone has said God has placed some "rests" in life's music. This attitude is reached only by a daily walk with God.

We make plans, but (as Joe says) when the action starts, things may not go the way we planned, and we're down to our training. I *plan* to spend my retirement years, if I live, in writing and related activities. But even now I condition myself for the possibility that God may have other plans for me. Could I joyously accept his will if I should be incapacitated?

I remember the night in 1949 when Clint and I learned that our baby Elliot would have to undergo a spinal tap to determine whether or not he had polio. His right arm appeared to be paralyzed, and we were most fearful of the result of the test.

After the doctor left our house, and before we went to the hospital, we went, hand in hand and holding Elliot, back into the bedroom and sat down on the side of the bed. I can't remember that we prayed audibly, yet I know we both prayed. It was as automatic as a reflex. We knew God was the only source of help. I was twenty-four and Clint was twenty-seven. This being our first encounter with tragedy in our little family, it couldn't have been sorrow that trained us.

No, in our moment of tragedy we acted on our training. Like Timothy, we had from childhood learned the Holy Scriptures. Both of us had observed our parents as they demonstrated their faith on a daily basis. We had seen that they turned to God in their trouble. When we established our own home, we never discussed whether or not we'd have Bible reading and prayer and hymns in our home. We just did.

During the three months that Elliot was in the Sister Kenny Institute, I knelt down many times and poured out my anguish to God. One time I felt God so near it was as though a heavy dew lay around me, a pressure like a hand on my head. Since then I have never doubted that his grace will always meet my crisis.

Recently I heard a statement over the radio which seemed to embody this truth: "The will of God will never lead you where the grace of God cannot keep you."

Crises of personality occur, too, which can be avoided to a great extent by doing our spiritual roadwork. We may have a quick temper, a cutting tongue, easily hurt feelings, a tendency to deceive, dirty minds. We say, "That's just the way I am." We should say, "That's the way I am *naturally*." The provision has been made for us to live above our natural state and draw on the nature of Christ to overcome our inherent tendencies.

14

It does take time to be holy. If we would just slow down a bit. If we would allow Christ to soften our thoughts, our words wouldn't pour out in venom. If we discipline ourselves in this manner, we will be able to control ourselves even when we have to react in a hurry.

Proverbs 31 speaks of the virtuous woman as having the law of kindness in her tongue. This might be a law she has imposed on herself and does not break. Or it might be a law so ingrained in her by training that it has become natural to her.

Frazier says that if you cheat on your roadwork in the dark, you'll be found out later under the lights. The reverse is also true. If you've been faithful in cultivating your spiritual resources, in time of crisis your "roadwork" will be evident.

For as you know him better, he will give you, through his great power, everything you need for living a truly good life: he even shares his own glory and his own goodness with us! And by that same mighty power he has given us all the other rich and wonderful blessings he promised; for instance, the promise to save us from the lust and rottenness all around us, and to give us his own character. So, dear brothers, work hard to prove that you really are among those God has called and chosen, and then you will never stumble or fall away. 2 Peter 1:3, 4, 10, TLB

Father, help us to appropriate all that is ours in Christ, that we may be able to stand in the day of trouble or testing, your Holy Spirit helping us. Amen.

Tents and Toes

It was mid-July, I was pregnant, and had three children under the age of six. As if that weren't enough for any mother to cope with, all three of them were now clamoring for me to "Please, put up the tent, Mommy."

Grudgingly, I went to the basement and found the moldy old scout tent and the spikes, carefully kept over my husband's workbench. With the eager help of every one of my own, plus several neighborhood children, I drove the spikes into the ground, got the pole to stand up enough to support the point of the tent, then tied the ropes to a stake.

As I hoisted my heavy self up and walked back to the porch, I stumbled over the rope. I caught myself for a moment, but still fell hard and headlong to the ground. In catching myself, my bare toes struck the concrete blocks at the base of the steps. At least a dozen children stood over me solicitously asking, "Are you all right?" I raised myself slowly, assuring them I was — just to keep them from worrying and trailing me into the house. I stood up and limped in. My toe really hurt.

I lowered my swollen body down onto the davenport and started to sob. I had landed hard and felt really shaken up. I didn't worry too much about my unborn baby — he was well cushioned. It was hot, fat, sore *me* that worried me. The July heat and the demands of each day were just too much for me. Defeat overwhelmed me. I hated myself and the bitterness I felt.

How that toe hurt! It turned blue in a matter of minutes, swelling to twice its size. I limped through the day. Night finally came and I prepared the children for bed. After the last trip to the bathroom for a drink of water for a parched little mouth, my responsibilities were over, hopefully, for the night. I went right to bed.

We needed the window fan for the heat, but the draft hurt my toe. I covered it with a sheet, wincing with pain. My husband went to sleep, but I lay there thinking.

"God," I questioned, "how can I be a good mother tomorrow with this sore toe? You know, I wasn't doing too well before, when only the heat bothered me." I lay there and waited, quite sure that God agreed with me so far. "What I'm asking for, Father, is special help to be a good mother tomorrow even if it's hot and no matter how much my toe hurts. I want to be an overcomer."

I slept.

A sleepy voice called from the adjoining room. "Mommie, I have to go poddee."

I got up, helped him to the bathroom, and tucked him back in his crib. In leaving his room, I bumped my toe against a wandering shoe. "Ouch," I muttered, and then realized that it hadn't hurt very much at all. I went back to bed. My toe wasn't hurting. I pulled up a sheet. Still no pain.

The next morning I stood up free of pain. The swelling of the toe had gone down, but it looked awful. Still black and blue, it looked as if it might be a permanent reminder of how bruised it had been.

I hadn't asked for the pain to be taken away — only that I might be able to stand it.

That day even the heat didn't bother me much. It seemed I had a new relationship with my Father. Perhaps he felt I was being tested more than I was able to bear.

Even though the pain was gone, the toenail stayed

blue and eventually came off, painlessly. As I marveled at this answer to prayer, it seemed God was telling me that he studies our motives. If his purpose can be accomplished in our lives without severe trials, he'll take them away.

When his purpose is accomplished, he removes the thorn in the flesh. That little grain of faith I used that night in the midst of my defeat and pain may have been exactly what he wanted to produce in me by that experience. When I showed my desire to live above frustration and defeat, he was able to take away the pain. But he left the blue toenail as a reminder through the rest of that long, hot, pregnant summer.

Him that overcometh will I make a pillar in the temple of my God, and he shall go no more out: and I will write upon him the name of my God, and the name of the city of my God, which is new Jerusalem, which cometh down out of heaven from my God: and I will write upon him my new name. Revelation 3:12

Lord, help me to be an overcomer today. Help me to realize that circumstances need not control my joy and peace because your grace is sufficient for me. Amen.

Saturday Night

My husband set Grace's shoes to one side and picked up another pair: "And these are Elliot's," he said aloud. I looked up, a little surprised.

Clint was giving the children's shoes their weekly polishing in preparation for going to church. With a tender look and voice, he then added, "As I polish each pair of shoes I think of each of the kids and pray for them."

That Saturday night I realized that to Clint the shoe polishing was more than the chore I'd thought it was. While I handled the children's clothing as part of my work, Clint's only regular job connected with their clothes was this Saturday night ritual.

I started thinking more about the children as I washed and ironed and mended. "This pretty dress of Grace's — help her desire inward beauty as she wears it." "O God, while Elliot is wearing this shirt, keep him honest." (Eight years old, Elliot was having trouble with lying.)

Later, when Grace was at the University of Minnesota, Elliot and Nella at Minnehaha Academy, Brian at Trinity Junior High School, and David at Powderhorn Christian School, I often prayed for their physical and moral protection. "O Father, put a hedge around Grace as so many philosophies crowd in on her."

Today, the piano top is lined with high school graduation pictures in need of dusting. As I hold each picture, I look at the faces of my children and implore God for the adult needs of each one. I pray that Grace, now married to Larry, and so very happy, will know with her husband that deeper dimension that

comes to a marriage when Christ is at the center. Elliot, in Sears management training: "You go ahead of
him and lead him to the place of your choice." Nella,
now married to Rick in the Lord, and teaching Mexican-
Americans Spanish and English: "Be with her, Father,
on a moment-by-moment basis. May they see Jesus in
her." Brian, still in college, engaged to lovely Terri:
"Help him to build his life on a sure foundation." How
thankful I am that nothing happens to any of them by
chance, but that everything is under the personal direction of their loving Father.

Then there's David — thirteen years old. He polishes
his own shoes and most of his clothes drip dry without
ironing. But he's still at home for us to guide a few
more years. Where his life will take him, we don't
know. We do know that our time for training is very
short. When he sets out into the open water, there'll
be no point in shouting directions from the shore.

When that time comes, we will continue to pray.
And to think that Almighty God, Creator of the universe,
Sustainer of stars and planets, hears us!

Salt

It must be twenty years ago, but I still blush
when I think of it.

I was a member of a ladies' Bible study
group of our church. One member had
brought a guest named June whom most of us knew.
She'd visited before and we had met her on other oc-

casions as well. When the Bible lesson started, this visitor sat down at my left.

During the discussion of the lesson, a certain young woman expressed her opinion a few times. This girl always irritated me. I sat there thinking how phony she acted. She put on airs and talked artificially, I thought. I turned to the visitor at my side and whispered, "I can't stand her!"

I expected her to smile or nod agreement with me. Instead, a look of horror sprang into her large brown eyes. I knew at once I'd spoken unwisely.

The following morning I got a telephone call. A very good friend wanted to talk to me about something. "When we were doing dishes after the meeting last night, June stayed back because she was riding with Kay. Well, I can't believe that you would do a thing like this — or rather say a thing like this —"

I felt myself get weak.

She went on, "I'll just have to tell you about it. June was so perturbed about something she claims you said. She says that when Ann was talking you whispered to her, 'I can't stand her!' I find it hard to believe you'd say that to a visitor, but she insists that you —"

A terrible lump hit my stomach. "I did it. I said that. I can't believe it either, but there's no point in denying it. What can I do about it?"

"Well, June said if Christians gossiped even during a Bible lesson —"

I blushed a hot, stinging red. June was a nominal Christian and I had offended her soul. "I'll call her. I can't undo what I did, but I'll tell her I made a terrible mistake."

I called June. She was gracious, saying she sometimes spoke hastily herself. She certainly could understand. Goodness, yes.

June never returned to that circle as long as I went there. To my knowledge, she has never become active in any church although she's a member of one.

Matthew Henry said, "Salt is a remedy for unsavory meat but there is no remedy for unsavory salt." I fear that my salt that night many years ago wasn't very salty.

Salt is good for all sorts of things. It removes stains and bad odors; it enhances flavor and prevents mildew; it removes bitterness from rancid coffee makers; it soaks loose burned-on food in a pan; it preserves food.

Christ said we're the salt of the earth. Do we rectify situations as hard to remove as grape-juice stains in a linen cloth? Do we sweeten the atmosphere when bitterness and evil abound? When someone is burned spiritually, do we help "clean him up" again? Do we add a pleasing flavor preserving good and preventing bad situations?

It's true no remedy exists for unsavory salt. But when our "salt loses its savor," Jesus can give us salty salt again.

I confessed my sin to God and he forgave me. I learned a lesson.

If we confess our sins, he is faithful and just to forgive us our sins, and to cleanse us from all unrighteousness. 1 John 1:9

Father, may this woman I offended so grievously many years ago turn to you with her whole heart. May this painful experience work for her good as well as mine, according to your word. Thank you for forgiving me and teaching me a lesson. Amen.

22

Celebration

My neighbor smiled. "It's my birthday today. I'm eighty-two years old."

Her eyes glowed through her glasses. Her face, once fat, was now thin. Her lips had to protrude to cover her dentures, which seemed too large for her face. Her pink scalp showed through her silver hair, which she had drawn back in a poorly-made French roll. Disobedient wisps strayed from it, falling around her ears.

"All the children are coming today," she continued, her weak voice almost trailing off at times. "I don't suppose Jane will be able to come. She is *so busy*. Why, she must be busier than I ever was when I had all my children, even the twins. Why, I never washed on Sunday, but Jane says she *has* to wash on Sunday."

Raising her head to see me better, and nodding encouragement, she asked, "Are you a Lutheran, too?" Somewhat sheepishly I admitted I wasn't. I felt she would have liked me better if I'd been Lutheran.

"I've been a Lutheran all my life," she stated proudly. "I remember the day I was confirmed. We all had to say Psalm 23. I still love that Psalm."

We were silent for some time. My neighbor appeared to be listening for something.

"Is George back?" she asked.

"No. He left only a half hour ago. He had several errands and I told him not to hurry."

George, her bachelor son, who had hired me to stay with his mother, seemed like her only child. I knew she had six more, in our city and in other parts of the country, but I'd never met any of them. (In this case, the philosophy seemed to be "Let George do it.")

23

The sun slipped behind my house across the street. Suddenly it seemed the day had disappeared, taking with it some of the cheer of the living room.

Distress clouded her countenance. "I can't understand it. Did you see us move to this house? For thirty years, we lived at 4652 Pine Street. I don't know why we had to come here."

She had risen from her chair and was moving toward the kitchen. Her feet didn't seem to go where she aimed them, and she almost tripped. I steadied her, hoping she'd soon find another chair. As we approached the kitchen, she asked, "Do you like coffee?" With a twinkle in her eye she added, "I'm crazy about it myself."

"Yes, I love coffee. I'll help you make it."

While I made the coffee, she busily investigated the cupboard from which she had been barred during a long illness. Her arthritic fingers, now bony and bent, opened one canister after another.

"I didn't bake any cookies," she said apologetically. Her hunt for sweets had produced three tea crackers and several fig newtons, which clinked as they hit the plate, already occupied by three sugar lumps.

Now in a festive mood, she asked, "How's the coffee?"

"It's ready. I'll get some cups. But first, why don't you sit down?"

"Yes, I'll sit down," she said patiently, as though indulging me in this notion I seemed to have that she might fall. Instead of sitting in the chair next to the cupboard where she stood, she shuffled around the table to the other side, in order to sit in a certain place.

She bowed her head briefly, then stole a shy smile at me saying, "Isn't this nice? That we can have this little party together today?" I agreed. I wouldn't have missed it for anything.

"It's my birthday today," she said again. "I'm eighty . . . seven years old. I've been a Lutheran all my life."

She became silent again, listening. "Is that the mailman? I believe it is. Will you please get the mail?"

Patiently, I showed her again the mail I'd brought into the house when I arrived. Shopping bills, advertisements, no letters. "The children are all coming today. I suppose that's why they didn't write," she said.

As darkness settled over the house, her mental darkness appeared to grow deeper.

"I can't understand it," she said. "That kitchen prayer on the wall is just like mine, and that calendar is just like mine, but —"

"You're at home, dear neighbor," I soothed. "See, this is your house." Pointing to the next room, I said, "Those pictures on the wall, aren't they all your children?"

She smiled tolerantly at me, nodding a little. "Yes, those are my pictures. George always tells me too that I'm at home."

Dunking her far-from-fresh fig newton in her coffee, she managed to get part of it to her mouth, but lost most of it in her coffee and on the bib of her apron. Taking her spoon, she fastidiously cleaned it up.

Now in a confidential whisper she said, "Isn't it scandalous how late the people of this house sleep? Here it's almost suppertime and they haven't stirred!" I nodded as pleasantly as I could.

Hoping to bring her back to straight thinking, I asked, "Did John come yet?" John, her very successful son, a consultant engineer, had written he hoped to see her soon on one of his trips through our city.

"Yes. He came last night. But I was gone to a party. I missed him completely!" Turning to look right into my eyes, she asked, "Isn't that a shame?"

I agreed. Who wouldn't? I wondered what made her think she had missed such a long-anticipated visit from her favorite and youngest son.

"I'm tired," she admitted wearily. "I guess I'll go to bed." She shuffled to the pantry where she took off her apron, feeling all over it first for the pocket, from which she drew a paper napkin. Wiping her mouth very hard, she restored the napkin to the pocket. Then she carefully hung the apron on a hook beside four other limp aprons, each of which testified to being as tired as she, and almost as old.

I walked right beside her, every step, catching her as she lost her balance from time to time. She walked through the dining room, explaining each picture to me. For a moment, as she talked about the far-distant past, and about her family, her mind seemed clear.

"This plant is eighteen years old. I started it with a shoot from a spray that was on my husband's casket," she remarked. She picked up household articles, looked at them, and laid them down in another place, apparently out of the well-formed habit of tidying up the house a bit before going to bed. She finally reached the stairs. With the use of the handrail, she was able to pull herself up.

At the top, she said "Shhh! The President and his wife are sleeping in that bedroom. They got in real late last night — all dressed up." Seeing that I was impressed, she went on, "She never speaks a word to me, and I've known her all my life."

"Who was she before she was married?" I inquired, wondering who had achieved such station in life.

"Oh," she said nonchalantly, "they used to have the lumberyard back in Pleasantville."

Preparing her for bed was a long project. Finally, she sat down on the edge of the bed. As she leaned back, I picked up her stiff legs, her feet swollen and blue at the ankles, and placed them on the bed. Then I lifted her at the shoulders and arranged her pillow at the head. Her blue nightie with ruffles gave her a little-girl look, her face angelic in its silver frame. Her eyes fell shut.

"Good night, dear neighbor," I whispered. "Sleep well." She raised her lips to me and I kissed her.

"Yes, good night," she said, trying to smile, but almost too weary. "I have to rest well, because it's my birthday tomorrow. All the children are coming, and they *always* take my picture with my cake. I'm going to be eighty . . ."

Her mind seemed to grope for the proper figure. I caressed her hair. "Yes, you'd better get a good rest."

Before going downstairs, I couldn't resist a peek into the bedroom occupied by the "President and his wife." I flicked on the light. Everything looked sanely back at me — the row of lysol bottles, packages of bathroom tissue — the storeroom.

I went back downstairs to do up the "party" dishes just as George returned from his errands.

"Your mother has been talking about her birthday a lot lately. Just when is her birthday?"

"Saturday, the third of April," he replied.

"I'd like to send her a cake. Is the family getting together?" I asked. There were several pictures about the dining room of previous celebrations, so I didn't consider my question out of order.

"I haven't heard of any such plans," he said, a little embarrassed, and added, "There's a feud going on in the family."

So that was it. What could I do? My old neighbor lived only for attention from her children, and apparently little would be forthcoming.

Saying good night to him, I left for home. "Fine time for a family feud!" I thought. "It's her birthday, and it may be her last. God forgive them. Oh, God, forgive them." Tears stung my eyes as I searched for the keyhole.

The Pledge

A friend told me of one particularly hard year she and her husband had gone through. Their children were small, and their only income was from odd jobs her husband was able to find. Their bills mounted.

One Sunday evening Dean stayed at home with the children. That was the night the pledge cards were to be turned in at church. Alice hadn't even discussed with Dean how much they should pledge. They had nothing left over after buying a minimum of food and clothing. They were a month behind in their rent. How could they pledge?

Alice sat in church chewing her pencil and looking at the card laid out on her Bible on her lap. She wanted to pledge. She deeply yearned to help the missionaries and her church. But what about the bills? Did she have a right to use money for the church which could be used to pay their creditors? She didn't think so.

As she was about to tuck the card back into her Bible, a phrase leaped into her mind: "For after these things do the Gentiles seek."

What? She tried to think of the rest of that verse.

She opened *Good News for Modern Man* to the Sermon on the Mount. Here she read in Matthew 6: "Your Father in heaven knows that you need all these things. Instead, give first place to His Kingdom and to what He requires, and He will provide you with all these other things. So do not worry about tomorrow; it will have enough worries of its own."

Alice read it again. Had she been reversing Christ's teaching and thinking like the unsaved world — giving first place to the gathering of sufficient material goods to live and *then* giving thought to the Kingdom?

But how could she practice Christ's teaching right now? Maybe a dollar a week. She'd no sooner thought of the dollar a week but she found herself thinking of what a dollar a week would buy for the children. Oranges and lettuce. Four dollars a month would help pay the dentist . . . the rent. No. She didn't want to think that way. Could she — dared she — pledge a dollar a week?

Was a dollar a week enough? She shrank at the thought of making it more. How much should she pledge anyway? Besides, what would Dean say?

She read the passage in Matthew 6 a third time, this time from the King James Version: "Seek ye first the kingdom of God, and his righteousness; and all these things shall be added unto you."

How would she know how much to pledge?

The tithe. She had been taught that the tithe was the minimum. But on what could they tithe? They had no fixed income.

Alice guessed in the absence of a fixed income, she'd have to start with their fixed indebtedness. She had some idea of how much money they had to have every single month in order to keep afloat. She put down a hundred dollars for rent. Then she quickly figured the total of their other debts and the amount they should expect to pay on them every month. She estimated a grocery bill that would include oranges and lettuce for the children, and meat three times a week.

After she computed the total of what would be needed for one month, she figured what the tithe on that would come to. This figure she added to the total. Then she prayed: "Lord, we need these things. I'm going to pledge you a tithe of the amount we need in order to meet our obligations and keep a roof over our heads. From here on it's up to you."

She filled out her card: $20, Missions; $20, General Fund; Total per month, $40.

It was years later that Alice told me about this act of faith. "You know," she said, "God never once failed to give us enough to meet that pledge and to make payments on our debts."

Lord, give us faith that will dare to make a commitment based on your promise. Amen.

Saved from Death

My oldest brother had an incurable, inoperable tumor. After two weeks of cobalt daily, it had shrunk to half its size. He went back for more cobalt. We asked God for healing. Finally a set of x-rays showed no tumor at all. Our prayer had been heard. He was healed.

Suppose you heard of a man on his deathbed who

prayed to be saved from death. If you then learned that he died the next day, would you say his prayer had been heard? I've been a church member all my life and have heard many testimonies, but I've never heard one person say, "I prayed for deliverance from a horrible experience. The Lord heard my prayer, and I went through it the next day."

We tend to consider a man saved from death only if he gets well. Without doubting the wisdom or love of God for taking a person in death, we seldom regard a man's death as an answer to his prayer for delivery from death.

It surprises us, therefore, to read in Hebrews 5:7 that when Christ was a man he begged God with strong crying and tears to save him from death . . . *and was heard.* How can the writer say that Christ was heard *when he died the next day?*

My brother's cancer returned. For six months, we had rejoiced in healing. Then back to our knees again in petition. Would disease be the victor this time? How many times could he be saved from death?

If Christ was heard when he prayed that he might be delivered from death even though he died the next day, there must be but one real delivery from death.

Matthew Henry, in his commentary on this portion of Hebrews, points out that we may have many recoveries from sickness, but we are never saved from death *until we are carried through it.*

Christ was heard: he was supported in his agonies; he was carried through death and delivered from death by a glorious resurrection.

Every brush with death, every narrow escape, means only respite from death. Only those who have passed through the door Death may enter Life. No other way exists to get to that place of joy where there is no cause for tears. No other way to find that place of health. No other way to dwell in that land of life.

> So when my latest breath shall rend the
>   vail in twain
> By death shall I escape from death and
>   life eternal gain.[1]

My brother died on August 14, 1971. "We are not afraid, but are quite content to die, for then we will be at home with the Lord" (2 Corinthians 5:8, TLB).

The Decision

A young man is hitchhiking on Interstate 94 this morning. And here's a woman who's crying inside.

It was only twenty-four hours ago that our pastor called. "Ruth, I'm going to ask you something and I want you to be absolutely honest with me, O. K.?"

I promised.

"Yesterday a fellow came into the church. He was very unhappy — almost desperate. I prayed with him and he received Christ. He has quite a past, and now he wants to start over. I'll be honest with you, too. He's been in a hospital for alcoholism, but he says he

---

[1]"Forever with the Lord" by J. S. Fearis, *Winnowed Anthems,* Hope Publishing Company, Copyright 1894 by Henry Date.

wants to be completely rid of his bad habits. He needs a place to stay."

"And you remembered that our house is gradually emptying out."

He chuckled. "Right."

"You're aware that we still have David at home. He's thirteen."

"Yes, I thought of that."

"Where would he be coming *from?* What sort of place is he moving out of?" I envisioned a flop-house. Bedbugs.

"He's in a halfway house right now. He's a clean, well-groomed fellow."

I'd pictured the worst of the counter culture. "How old is he?"

"Twenty-nine."

My own oldest child is twenty-six.

"Clint, of course, is at work, and we won't have much chance to talk about this until later this evening since I teach tonight. But I'm interested and I think Clint will be too."

"Call me later tonight then. There's more I can tell you if you're both interested in giving him a home. I'll say this. I got John Road to give him a job, so he could pay his own way with you."

Clint and I talked over coffee when he returned from work. He was surprisingly open to the idea.

"It'll mean we can't leave David at home alone as we've been doing," I warned. This had been the first winter we hadn't brought in an outsider for David when we went out for an evening. David enjoyed playing his instruments and liked having the house to himself. But this would change if we brought in this questionable character.

"What would be reasonable to ask for room and

board?" Clint wondered. I had no idea. This was the week of the meat boycott. Food prices were at an all-time high. It was costing three of us as much to eat as it had ever cost us to feed the family of seven when they were all at home.

I went off to teach my class in Writing and thought about this young man and the possible effect of taking him in. I loved my privacy with my family. We couldn't very well offer this former alcoholic, this recent convert, a home, and then require him to stay in his room. If he was going to board with us, it would mean no more family suppers. I imagined him staying on well into the evening, sitting in my favorite chair right next to Clint, under my favorite light. Where would I sit? Across the living room under the poor light, I supposed. And I dared say, every time Clint and I would want to watch television late at night he'd be there.

On the other hand, I liked the thought of sharing some of our times with him. It thrilled me to think he'd sit with us during our family devotions and hear the Bible reading morning and evening. I knew Clint's prayers would strengthen him as they always did me.

Then I remembered that Clint's work took him out of town periodically for several days at a time. In fact, the next week, he was to be gone three days. I shuddered. And me in the house alone with David and this man.

The next minute, I was imagining him as a friendly, warm-hearted lad who'd take the place of my own sons grown and gone. "Run this to the basement for me a minute, will you?" I'd say, and he'd say, "Sure." Just like my own. It'd be nice having him around when Clint was gone.

When I got home from class, Clint and I took up the discussion once more. "What would you think of $25 a week for room and board, if he uses the boys' room as is?" Clint asked. He added, "He might eat as much alone as the three of us do together, you know."

"Maybe $30 if we give him Nella's room until we get the gang in here for her wedding in June." We were silent. "I wonder if he smokes. I'd hate to have Nella's mattress filled up with smoke." We couldn't decide on anything.

"Let's call pastor and see what more he can tell us."

Clint took the upstairs phone. Pastor was waiting for our call. "You're still interested. Good. On my way home from board meeting tonight I was thinking, 'What a burden I've put on those people.' "

"Tell us more about this man, pastor."

"He has a rather sordid past. He's been in St. Louis and Chicago. He was raised by an aunt and his grand-parents. He was made to feel no good. He ran away from home early and joined the army. He slit his wrists while in the army, but he said he did this to get psychiatric attention he felt he needed."

I swallowed hard. If we took this guy in, we'd be due for a sanity test ourselves. With a thirteen-year-old son in the house? Never!

Pastor continued. "He's got a police record for theft. He says he did this to get in jail in hopes of getting help. He was pretty far gone and very desperate when he came in here yesterday afternoon."

My eyes went to the buffet where I had a dozen or more March of Dimes envelopes, delivered to me after mothers had made their march. I wondered what Clint was thinking.

Pastor still spoke. It seemed this man had no end of serious problems. "He admits to having engaged in male prostitution but says he did it only when he was way down and had absolutely no money. He had no desire for it and would never do it again."

Clint coughed on that one.

This could all be past if he'd become a Christian. Clint asked my next question, "Did his conversion yesterday seem genuine?"

"I'll say this. I went out on a limb when I asked John to give him work. I can't judge his heart, but I'd like to see him given a chance to prove himself. I did think he was a little pushy. He seemed to want action right now. Of course, I might be that desperate, too, in his shoes."

Pushy, desperate, a thief, an alcoholic, a prostitute — we'd be fools to give that man a key to our house.

But God was saying, "Wait a minute."

While pastor and Clint talked, I caught a picture of myself. I glimpsed the Ruth that God sees. Then I remembered that the sinless Jesus died for me, unlovely and unlovable. I had always been a Christian. I couldn't remember a day I hadn't known Christ as my Savior. As I listened to pastor describe this sordid life, I realized what I'd been spared. I thought of my own five children. They had also been introduced to Jesus at an early age. Surely we were blessed to have been so gloriously delivered from that kind of sin.

Then I thought, What if that were Elliot — or Brian — or David? This young man's mother had died young. What would she have thought, how might she have felt, had she seen the degradation into which her son had slipped?

Clint was saying, "We'll have to discuss it some more. We'll let you know for sure tomorrow morning. When would he move in?"

"I'm sure he'd like to move in right away."

"We'll call you."

36

We both hung up and met in the living room. Clint said, "It's going to mean we really trim our life style. We can't ever leave David alone with him, even to watch television."

"Let's try it for a month. Let's tell pastor we can't help him long because of David, but we'd like to give the fellow a chance to get his feet on the ground. He'll make some friends around church. He'll have time to get an apartment of his own."

"We'll tell pastor tomorrow." Clint picked up the paper.

I didn't dare remind him that I'd be alone with this former criminal and pervert the following week. To God I said, "Please, please, when I meet him, take away my fear."

I didn't rest well last night. I dreamed I came into the living room and a strange man stood up from my chair and greeted me. His pockets were bulging with March of Dimes packets. Shock and fear gripped me.

This morning I went back to bed to get a few more hours of sleep. The telephone woke me. It was pastor.

"The whole thing's off. He called at two o'clock this morning and said to forget it. He said he was going back to Chicago. He said he'd be standing at the entrance to I-94 this morning to hitch a ride to Chicago."

"He's gone then?"

"He's gone."

All morning, my thoughts have been with that young man. I picture him standing in the chill, taking a ride with this one and that one, each taking him farther into his old life.

Grace

In 1946, my husband and I named our first child "Grace." It means "unmerited favor," "undeserved blessing."

Years have shown me more of the meaning of grace. One minister said, "Grace couldn't be defined. God had to act it out on Calvary."

John Newton, hymnwriter who lived from 1725 to 1807, wrote "Amazing grace, how sweet the sound/ That saved a wretch like me! I once was lost, but now am found/Was blind, but now I see."

Like Newton, I realize I couldn't have come to God by myself. His grace found me and gave me spiritual sight.

In the second verse he says, " 'Twas grace that taught my heart to fear/and grace my fears relieved. How precious did that grace appear/the hour I first believed."

This reminds me of the healthy "fear" I had of my father. No little girl ever adored her daddy more than I did mine, but I feared him too. His stern look was more to be dreaded than thunderstorms, and I trod circumspectly lest I should displease him. We were closely bound to each other. I desired his approval so much that I seldom risked losing it by disobeying him. His love and the sweet fellowship we enjoyed gave me respect for his wishes. Being a normal child, I sometimes deserved his black look. But because my penitence for wrongdoing brought instant forgiveness and a happy countenance, I also know what Newton meant when he said, "And grace my fears relieved."

The song continues: "Through many dangers, toils, and snares/I have already come."

Some of us challenge Satan's ingenuity more than others. He has a ready package of temptations to snare us. While the church doesn't legislate to the extent it once did, worldly amusements are still favorite devices of Satan to possess our minds and bodies. If he's unsuccessful with these, he dips into his bag for more original ideas fitted to the individual.

When our children were little, I encouraged them to read and discouraged them from watching much television. Today they all love books. But when I read modern fiction, I sometimes wish the kids were watching television instead. At least TV is to some extent censored. Not every book will make one a better person; some will weaken our spiritual resources against sin. If a writer is skillful, we may find ourselves sympathizing with characters who are violent or adulterous or drunken. This is the insidious evil of some fiction.

Satan is clever. We aren't all tempted in the same way. Some of us feel less pull from the world, but Satan doesn't leave us alone because of that. One woman who suffered severe mental depression began to note improvement almost immediately after she publicly stated that she believed it was Satan's last tool in his bag of tricks. She explained that she had never been drawn toward the world; she had served God to the best of her ability in her home and church. Yet depression had taken away her joy. Having named Satan as the instigator of her misery, she found that he left her, at least for a while.

Yes, "through many danger, toils, and snares/I have already come: 'Tis grace hath brought me safe thus far/ and grace will lead me home."

Why, God?

"Rejoice in the Lord alway."

Forced to turn my attention to our pastor, I smarted under his kind, appealing smile. Rev. Rikkers appeared to be beckoning us to a higher level, one he had reached. "What made him choose that theme today?" I questioned. I turned my face toward the wall. The sun streamed in through the "Christ in Gethsemane" stained-glass window.

I turned again toward the pulpit.

"Yes, *alway!* Not *in spite of,* but *because of* the special attention you have received from God. In *everything* give thanks. Not in *doubt,* but in *certainty* that he does as he does out of the love of his heart. Give thanks *always* for *all* things."

Disbelief swept through me. "It wouldn't be Christian to give thanks for such a terrible thing. If God had touched *my* body, perhaps I could come to the place where I could be thankful. But. . . ." Tears flooded my eyes. The unerasable picture of Elliot, my infant son, whom we had just brought home from the Kenny Polio Institute the week before, flashed upon my mind.

Three months earlier, grief stricken but full of hope for his cure, we had taken him there. Bringing him home had crushed us. His right arm was still completely limp at the shoulder. Both legs were so tight it was doubtful he'd ever walk without braces.

"Give thanks for that?" I asked God.

Years slipped by. Years tedious with exercising, stretching, counting, and vibrating atrophied muscles and knocked-out nerves.

In time Elliot learned to walk. By stretching his legs,

we kept him walking, even though his leg muscles had seriously shrunk. He wore out his shoes before the store had a chance to bill us, yet the heel of the shoe remained in excellent condition, the trademark still intact.

Our family increased at the rate of one every two years. We never skipped Elliot's exercises in spite of the strain it laid upon us. At times it was excruciatingly painful to witness the daily reminder of unanswered prayer. "Stretch to the point of pain and beyond," the doctor had said. My husband and I often grew misty-eyed as together we worked him over, one holding his hips in place firmly, while the other pulled the leg over as far as it would go.

Two periods daily, while vibrating the arm, I prayed in rhythm, "Lord, heal; Lord, heal; Lord, heal."

Would God heal? What if it weren't his will? I was tormented by the thought of my baby going into life with a paralyzed arm and weak legs. It took years to reconcile myself to the possibility that God might not see fit to heal.

While I never quit praying for healing of the arm, I somehow felt I had received God's answer and that it had been "No." Time made it possible for me to resign myself to this. Even after all possible surgery, the doctors said, he'd still have only 40 percent normal use of the arm.

Elliot had physical handicaps to be sure, but none in personality. He participated in everything boys his age did. He learned most things one to two years later than they, but he taught himself cheerfully and patiently, asking no pity, and expecting no favors. His attitude of love toward others caused him to receive much love from the world.

While I had formerly asked why it couldn't have been

41

I who had the handicap, now I admitted I could never have been as gracious about it as he.

As Elliot grew older, he occasionally drew me into discussions about the purposes of God. Through the years my sorrow had driven me to the Word of God many times and I had received many comforting answers from it. I had learned something about why God permits such distressing experiences as polio to come to his children.

One evening when Elliot wanted to talk, I leaned wearily against the post that joined the top to the bottom bunk. Elliot, now nine, climbed into the top bunk, his right arm hanging useless. This inadequacy in climbing must have caused him to bring up the subject. "Mother, why did God give me polio?"

I stiffened slightly. Careful now, I warned myself. You're very tired. You can't allow Elliot to sense any doubt of God's goodness.

"Well, son," I groped in my fatigue, "we can't blame God for your polio. But I suppose, knowing you and your whole life — I mean, knowing you from beginning to end, I suppose God thought you needed to have polio."

"What? What do you mean?"

I handled that badly, I rebuked myself. I tried again.

"If God had thought you would absolutely have to have two normal arms and two normal legs, he wouldn't have let you get polio, would he?" My own confidence surprised me.

"No, I s'pose not."

I searched my heart for a Bible verse. "It says in the Bible that Christ's strength is made perfect in our weakness. Where we are weak, he comes in with his strength to show us we can get along without strength of our own."

42

Elliot listened intently. Inspired by my words, I continued. "Elliot, God is your Father, and he loves you. He sees your whole life and you can be sure that there's something he wants to do for you that he can best do for you because you had polio. You must learn to listen for his voice in your life and to watch for his leading, so you don't miss the wonderful plan he has for you."

Elliot's rapt attention carried me on. "God's Word tells us that if we're his children, he tests us. If you are put through something hard to bear, that shows that God is dealing with you as a son. Elliot, not all of us have a permanent sign that we are God's child. *Consider your weak arm your badge of sonship.*"

Taking the arm tenderly in my hand, I said, "If you accept this from God as a sign that you're his child, someday you'll know why you had to go through life with this weakness. And always remember, in heaven your body will be perfect."

My words, meant to enlighten and comfort my son, reached way down into my own soul and turned on a light. I wanted to linger in that spot, fearful that to move might be again to enter into the shadows of anxiety.

Elliot had begun to pray. These words reached my ears: "Lord, thank you for my polio. I know you have a purpose for me. Help me to watch for your leading so I won't miss it. . . ."

I raised my face to his, and from his upper bunk, he bent down and kissed my wet cheek.

That evening, together with my son and leaning heavily on our Father, I took my first steps in "giving thanks always for all things."

My grace is all you need; for my power is strongest when you are weak. 2 Corinthians 12:9a, TEV

Father, thank you that you meet the doubts and anxieties of your children when they bring them to you. Thank you for that all-sufficient grace. Amen.

The Agnostic Who Sold Cemetery Lots

The man in my living room was selling cemetery lots. Since we didn't own any, I listened carefully to his sales talk. "This isn't operated for a profit," he said. "Should you want to sell any or all of it, you would have to sell it back to us. This cemetery is operated by a perpetual trust fund."

He looked about sixty years old, slim, graying, strong facial features, quite nice looking. "You should have lots before you have a death in your family, Mrs. Peterman," he urged. "When tragedy strikes is no time to go hunting for the proper place to lay to rest someone you love. A death shouldn't find you unprepared for this important decision."

Even though he looked at me so earnestly, my mind started to wander. Was he selling cemetery lots or making an evangelistic appeal? Since I couldn't make a decision about lots without my husband, I thanked him and promised to think about it.

Then as he got ready to go, I felt led to ask him to remain for just a moment. I pointed out to him that his daily work gave him a preoccupation with the physical aspects of death. I said we should make another even more important decision before death: where would we spend eternity? I asked him if he ever thought about this.

"Yes, I have," he said. "I'm, I guess, what you'd call an agnostic. I don't believe in heaven or hell. I'm not exactly against God or things like that. I guess I'm just not sure there is a God, like someone who's keeping track of what I do and all that. I'm doing the best I can. Maybe I figure heaven is here on earth if you live right."

Again my mind wandered. I seemed to see this man before the judgment seat of Christ. I heard him say, "I did the best I could. I wasn't exactly against you, but I just wasn't sure."

"Sir," I said, my voice trembling a little. "Your hair is turning gray. You have no assurance you'll live another day or hour. I beg you to study the Bible and turn to God. His Word tells us there is a hereafter and that where we spend it doesn't hinge on our intentions. Only those who believe Christ died for their sins will live with him forever. Don't let death find you unprepared!"

Tears came into my eyes and my voice broke. The man fled.

If I hadn't felt led to say what I had, I should have been quite embarrassed. We didn't buy cemetery lots. I've wondered ever since if that man heeded my warning. Even though that was about fifteen years ago, the Lord still sometimes prompts me to pray for him.

I have planted, Apollos watered; but God gave the increase. We are laborers together with God.

1 Corinthians 3:6, 9

Father, only you know if that man selling cemetery lots is still living and whether or not he turned to you. If he didn't, may someone still water that seed I planted many years ago. We know you are willing that all men should be saved. We trust you to give the increase if we are faithful in our witness. Amen.

Love Is Reason Enough

I went upstairs to make the beds. David, then four years old, soon followed, carrying his half-grown cat. Thinking he'd carried the cat upstairs to show it to me, I took it, but David reached for it again. "Did you come up here to show me the kitty?" I asked.

"No," he replied, "I just came to see you because I love you." That was reason enough for climbing the stairs with the kitty's extra weight.

I wondered what love felt like to a four-year-old. I envied the simplicity of soul that enabled him to be so forthright in telling how he felt. My mind went to various people who might be hungering for someone to reach out to them lovingly: those in prisons, young kids confused and trying to find a substitute for love, old people in nursing homes or living alone, individuals bereft of loved ones by death or divorce.

In Proverbs 31, which describes the virtuous woman, the writer says, "She stretcheth out her hand to the poor. Yea, she reacheth forth her hands to the needy."

Sometimes it's a long stretch from where we are to where the poor are. It may be a long reach to touch the physically needy. But the lonely and depressed are all about us.

At one time, my husband and I were made under-shepherds in our large church. The undershepherds' duty was to work "under" the pastors by calling on old and sick people in a given area of the city. Our church began this system in an effort to bring love to shut-ins and to make all the members active.

We stopped in, one Sunday afternoon, to visit an old lady whom we'd never met before. Her only child lived outside the U.S., so she had no children or grand-children to visit her. While we chatted with her, she seemed ill at ease. Conversation lagged, so I asked if she had any pictures of her family. She showed some to us, and then sat back in her chair and eyed us sus-piciously. She had so little to say that we started to feel ill at ease ourselves. After a few more attempts to bring some pleasure into her afternoon, we said we thought we'd better go. At this, no longer able to con-ceal her curiosity, she blurted out, "Didn't you come for money?"

When we had telephoned her we had explained who we were, but not realizing how seldom she received callers from the church, we hadn't properly explained our mission. From her question, we knew the under-shepherd ministry of our church was long overdue.

Today our society tends to help widows and orphans collect all the money coming to them and then leave them to work out their problems by themselves.

A friend of mine lost her mother when she and her brothers and sisters were young. She remembers that a neighbor lady used to bake bread for them every other day. This meant that this woman baked bread every day of the week in order to have enough for two families. The hand she reached forth to the needy was white with flour, but what she did said unequivocally, "I love you." Somehow, a pension check from the

47

Veterans Administration or Social Security doesn't convey that kind of caring.

People are lonely. Our smile, our handshake, the way we look into the eyes of people we meet — all of these give a message. Is it, "I love you"?

Love is its own excuse for doing.

Owe no man any thing, but to love one another: for he that loveth another hath fulfilled the law.

Romans 13:8

Father, the only way we can stay out of debt to our neighbor is to keep paying off the great debt of love we owe you. When we were far from you, strangers living in sin, you loved us and gave your Son for our sins. May our love for you overflow in love to our neighbor. Amen.

Love Story

 Vance and Roberta O'Day clung to each other and wept. Everything they had prayed and hoped for the past seven months was dashed.

The O'Days had agreed to have their baby's leg amputated, believing that if he grew up with an artificial limb he would have less of a handicap than if a useless appendage without an ankle or foot hung from his knee. But today the limb technicians had fitted the leg to little Patrick's stump, a little wooden leg with a lacer that went around the thigh and with shoulder and waist straps. In spite of the harness, the limb soon detached from the stump and dangled ludicrously.

This was the crudest device they had ever seen. It had no ankle, no foot action — and that harness would make a parachutist look well dressed! The baby would have to be fully undressed even to be diapered. Vance knew his son would never learn to walk with that limb.

When Patrick was born, Vance was already fifty years old; his wife was forty-two. They had no other children. Pat had come into the world with a congenital defect; one lower leg consisted only of tissue. Their doctor advocated early amputation.

Roberta was a registered nurse. Vance had been forced to leave medical school after six years of medical training during the depression, but had later taken both a physics and mechanical engineering degree. After seeing the monstrosity which had been attached to Pat's little stump, Vance felt that he could make a better one. With God's help, he set out to do it.

Vance left the defense firm where he was the senior mechanical engineer and became an unpaid apprentice to a limb maker.

Wood, rawhide, and steel were still used almost exclusively. Vance made many drawings and experimented with modern materials which showed potential for use in prosthetic devices. He made a plaster duplicate of Pat's stump, not just a drawing of the profile and face view of it as was being done by the limb makers.

He decided to try fiberglass and resins to make the socket for the stump. He baked the socket in his wife's oven for several hours, producing a strong chemical odor which hung in the house for hours. He then chiseled the plaster cast out of the socket, discarding the cast, which was no longer needed.

Vance made two prostheses in this fashion. They became Pat's first functional legs. On the second leg, Pat took his first steps and then walked totally unassisted fifteen days before he became ten months old!

Through the years, Vance devoted his life to improving his methods. He continued to provide Patrick with limbs as he grew larger. The limbs Vance made required no device to hold them on. Vance developed a foot that would do everything except wiggle its toes. He developed a knee socket that could be worn painlessly. He perfected a mechanical knee that could be as free as a pendulum or be locked stiff in an instant.

Today Pat is over six feet tall. In high school, he went out for sports and won a special award for accumulated service. He traveled with a well-known musical troupe for three summers, attending college during the school year. Now Pat is married and preparing for the ministry.

Vance has received two honorary doctorates as a result of his achievements in prosthesis. Presently he is working toward borrowing enough money to begin a school and franchise those who want to make limbs his way. It has already cost him $50,000 to get this far. He says he will retire only when others have been taught how to carry on his work on such a scale that any amputee desiring a good prosthesis may have one.

When Vance reviews his life, he thanks God for so completely qualifying him for his life's work before he himself knew what that would be. His knowledge of medicine, physics, and mechanical engineering has been put to use in developing what has been declared by many experts to be the most functional and attractive lower limb made. With this knowledge, Vance mixed faith and prayer. But the motivating force was his love for his son.

God so loved the world that he gave his only begotten
Son that whosoever believeth in him should not perish
but have everlasting life.   John 3:16

*Father, the story of Vance O'Day's love for his only son
reminds us again of how much you loved us. You
spared not your only Son but delivered him up as a
sacrifice for our sins. We can scarcely comprehend such
love. Amen.*

Why Act Like a Cripple?

"Shall I do it?" I inquired anxiously.

"I can!" came the irritated retort. "You
think I'm a cripple, don't you?"

According to ordinary standards, Elliot
was a cripple. His right arm had been completely paralyzed from the shoulder since infancy. Both of his legs
were tight and one was weak. But somehow he had
arrived at the age of fifteen considering himself quite
normal.

During his childhood, he rode a bike, played ball,
and worked. But this morning, when he seized the iron
carrier containing three glass gallon jugs of milk, to
help put away the groceries, I lost my "cool" and offered help. While Elliot had some physical evidence
that he was a "cripple," his attitude overcame the evidence.

The Bible says in Romans 6 that we are to consider
ourselves dead to sin and alive unto God. The King

James translation says, "Reckon yourselves to be dead indeed unto sin."

The evidence is forever present that we are spiritually crippled. We're handicapped persons — because of sin. Yet we're told to overcome the evidence by our attitude. The attitude is based on fact: that Christ died once and for all to sin, and is alive unto God.

I like that word *reckon* better than *consider* used in some newer translations. *Reckon* is a mathematical term used in accounting. There are no estimates, no maybe's, when you keep books. Not until you take in the money do you list it under "credits."

So enter it in the ledger: "Dead to Sin." And over in the next column: "Alive to God."

Are you defeated today? Take a fresh look at Romans 6. Were you baptized into the death of Christ, of which water is the symbol? If so, you've also been raised as he was to newness of life.

"Knowing this, that our old nature is crucified with him, that the body of sin might be destroyed, that henceforth you should not serve sin. . . . Now if we be dead with Christ we *believe* that we shall also live with him. . . . Likewise *reckon* ye also yourselves to be dead indeed unto sin, but alive unto God through Jesus Christ our Lord. Let not sin therefore reign in your mortal body. . . . Neither yield ye your members as instruments of unrighteousness unto sin: but *yield yourselves unto God,* as those that are alive from the dead."

Crippled? Not really. Not if you *know* and *believe* and *reckon,* and then *yield.*

But of him are ye in Christ Jesus, who of God is made unto us wisdom, and righteousness, and sanctification, and redemption. 1 Corinthians 1:30

Father, help me to receive everything provided for me in the death of my Savior. Don't let me accept less than the abundant life that comes with victory over my spiritual handicaps. Amen.

Is There Any Comfort for Parents?

The young man approaching the podium was introduced as "Don." Don had "lived LSD," had been converted, and was now going straight. We were at a workshop of the National Sunday School Convention in Minneapolis.

Don stood for a moment looking as though he might cry or run away. He was such an ordinary looking person, except for his piercing eyes, that I thought, "He could be anybody's son — even mine."

Lately, I had been asking myself, "Is there any comfort for parents?" I had heard of so many children who had virtually become enemies of their parents. Children and parents seemed to be on different channels — talking, even shouting, but not getting through to each other.

Don spoke: "Would you just pray with me a minute? I'm. . . ." He smiled a little stiffly.

"Dear Jesus, please help me now. I'm pretty scared. Help me tell these people some of the things I came here to tell them. Amen."

He came right to the point. "I suppose you're wondering what makes a kid go on LSD. When I was thirteen, I got in with the wrong kind of kids." His eyes met mine like bullets with a target. "Your kids' friends are important. I can't stress this enough."

He paused a moment, then pressed his fingertips to his temples, and shut his eyes. He wrinkled up his whole forehead, seeming to make a physical effort to push his thoughts into sequence.

"At my church where my folks went regularly, I didn't fit into the crowd. Nobody talked to me. I decided to go with my other friends who liked me."

So his folks went to church, even regularly. This could happen to my son or daughter, or to anyone else. "Belonging" is about all that matters to kids. Church kids can be awfully cliquey.

Don went on. "By the time I was sixteen, I was drinking four or five nights a week."

I gasped. At the age of sixteen? Where were his parents? Had they, fearing his rebellion, given him too much liberty?

Don continued, "When my friends started on grass and recommended it, I tried it too."

At this point of Don's talk, I remembered a little pamphlet I'd received from the Federal Bureau of Drug Abuse (*Drug Abuse: The Empty Life*). It warned: "Heavy or frequent use of liquor in a group usually paves the way for experiments with drugs. When the alcohol flows freely, you can consider it a danger sign."

Once more Don pushed his temples with the fingers of both hands and wrinkled his forehead. After a moment, he said, "My parents are both fine Christians."

I protested inwardly. "That can't be! Regular church people, maybe, but do the children of parents who personally know the Lord go so far into sin?" This was indeed a depressing workshop, informational but depressing.

Don rambled on, describing the mellow high from

"pot" and the hallucinations while under LSD. "Folks," he said, "guys who are on drugs are miserable. They're in a world of their own. They wish when you meet them on the street you'd say 'hi' or something. They want you, and they want Christ. If you speak to a fellow with long hair and he rejects you, you can be sure he's not living LSD."

The pamphlet had said: "Thousands of drug abusers live for years in the shadows of society — only half alive, only half free."

Finally, Don answered the question I'd been mentally asking. "You may wonder what brought me back. I had accepted Christ when I was younger. Now, when I was eighteen, I started searching. I was driving a truck when God said to me, 'Don, there's got to be something else.' I knew it was God showing me there was a better way for me. I invited Christ back and everything else left. I knew I'd go off drugs, but the first week the only thing I quit was smoking. It's been like hell the last six months. LSD affects your mind. You get very paranoid after using it a while. But with Christ, I know I can stay off drugs. Pray for me, will you?"

So it wasn't a person who influenced Don at all — it was *the* Person, the Holy Spirit of God. Don's early training, his early acceptance of Christ, had made him reachable by the Holy Spirit without human aid.

I remembered that Noah's sons were saved from the flood because each of them, by an act of will, stepped into the ark that Noah had prepared for the "saving of his house." The sons-in-law of Lot, who rejected the invitation to flee the fire and brimstone of God which was to descend on Sodom, were destroyed.

The invitation stands for parents *and their children* to go into the ark of safety — Christ Jesus. The parents "prepare the ark" with instruction and much prayer.

The Holy Spirit deals with the children, urging them to go into the ark with their parents. God is faithful.

This is my comfort as a parent.

Then Peter said unto them, Repent, and be baptized every one of you in the name of Jesus Christ for the remission of sins, and ye shall receive the gift of the Holy Ghost. For the promise is unto you and to your children. Acts 2:38, 39
Believe on the Lord Jesus Christ and thou shalt be saved *and thy house.* Acts 17:31

Father, help all Christian parents to trust you to keep your promises. Comfort parents, and oh, God, comfort the young people who are searching for you too. Amen.

Miracle in Malaya

 A missionary traveling in an unfamiliar region of the Malay Peninsula was surprised to learn that the governor of that province believed in Christ. He heard this story:

Thirty years earlier when the governor and his wife were mending some of the broken idols worshiped by their tribe, the governor stopped and called his wife's attention to his hand. Looking at his hand he exclaimed that surely his hand was a greater thing than these lifeless images they were mending. From that deduction, he took the next logical step: surely human beings, intelligent and creative, were greater than the pieces of wood and stone that they shaped into images and worshiped. "How absurd it is for us to worship these dead things, as if they could do anything for us!" he exclaimed. His wife said she'd often thought the same thing.

They decided no longer to worship the gods made with their own hands, but rather to destroy them. But what would they worship now? They agreed to worship the Being they were sure existed who was greater than man, who must have made man and the earth and the stars.

After some time, they heard about a man in the province who was selling a book. Somehow the governor felt that this book would be what he had waited for. He eagerly sent for the man and asked for the book. The man said: "This is the book that tells about the greatest Being in the universe." The governor bought it. It was a copy of the Christian Scriptures in his own language. He and his wife sat on the verandah for many hours while he read this wonderful book to her from the beginning.

When they came to Paul's sermon to the Athenians on Mars Hill, where he spoke of the people worshiping the "unknown God," the governor said, "Wife, we have been living in Athens for years!" Taught by the Holy Spirit alone, they came to know the true God and Jesus Christ whom he sent.

When the governor and his wife had ceased to worship idols they had told their people of their decision to worship the Being who created them and the world. Now they were able to formulate a more complete statement of faith.

The missionary was astounded to find that, without human aid, this Spirit-led governor of a tribe in the Malay Peninsula had comprehended the doctrine of the

Trinity and the Person of God. His creed read: "I believe in God, the Father of all things. I believe in Jesus Christ, the Son of God, as my Savior. I believe in the Holy Ghost as my Comforter and Teacher."

(The story above is documented in *The Message of Romans* by Robert C. McQuilkin (President, Columbia Bible College, Columbia, South Carolina), Zondervan Publishing House, Grand Rapids, Michigan, 1947.)

In reading the above account, I realized that I often underestimate the power of the Holy Spirit and the Word.

Once, when I handed a lady a tract, she received it cheerfully, saying, "Thank you. I was saved by a tract." It's possible that the person who gave her that tract won't know of her salvation until heaven.

We tend to think we have to convert people ourselves. We forget that the Word is a two-edged sword wielded by the Spirit of God. We're asked to plant and water. God gives the increase.

What if the Bible salesman hadn't gone to that province in the Malay Peninsula? Surely wherever people are living up to the light they have, God provides a way for them to get more light. It behooves us to obey when we are called.

How can they call on him if they have not believed? And how can they believe, if they have not heard the message? And how can they hear if the message is not preached, if the messengers are not sent out?

Romans 10:14, TEV

Lord, help us to be faithful in spreading your Word, trusting you to use it as you have promised when you said your Word will accomplish what you please and will prosper in the thing whereto you sent it. Amen.

Prayer is Personal

 On one of those rare Sunday mornings when the time seemed right for personal testimonies, one fellow in our adult class rose and said this:

"My father was very sick and when I said good-bye to him, I felt I wouldn't see him alive again. We traveled back to our home, my thoughts constantly with my father in prayer. Each night, when we went to bed, as I prayed for Dad, I asked God to waken me when Dad was dying so I could pray for his homegoing.

"A few nights later, a noise woke me out of a deep sleep. At first, in my sleepiness, I thought nothing of it. Then I remembered my father and only then did I remember I'd asked God to wake me so that I could pray for Dad's homegoing. I had no idea what had awakened me as everything was quiet now, but I just lay there and prayed for Dad. Ten minutes later, my sister telephoned me. When I heard her voice, I said, "Dad's gone, isn't he?" She said, "Yes, he just passed away." The next morning, I saw that the window shade had shot up during the night, and that must have been what God used to waken me."

This little story thrills me because it shows how personal our God is. He honored the faith of this man in what might seem a small thing, yet it was precious and meaningful to him. God gave personal attention to this request in such a definite way that there could be no doubt he did it.

How important it is to be personal with God.

When our youngest child, David, was in second grade, he had to miss school one day because he had a slight cold. In his prayer that night, he prayed, as he

59

did every night, for all the sick. "Take care of all the people in the hospitals and make them well, and all the people who are sick and not in the hospitals, please make them well, too." He then apparently remembered that he'd been out of school that day and he added, "That's me."

Jesus taught his disciples to pray in a personal way.

My Father who art in Heaven. Hallowed be thy name by me. Thy kingdom come, thy will be done through me on earth as it is done in heaven. Give me this day my daily bread and forgive me my trespasses as I forgive those who trespass against me. Lead me not into temptation but deliver me from evil for Thine, not mine, is the kingdom and the power and the glory forever. Amen.

Two Fathers

Nella was looking forward to her birthday party. We were planning to take her with her guests to the neighborhood park for a picnic. The night before, she knelt to pray. In praying about her party, she said, "If you want it to rain tomorrow — it's all right then. But I'd rather it didn't."

Her simple little statement has always illustrated for me what Paul meant when he said in Philippians 4, "Let your requests be made known unto God."

To hear adults pray, one might at times conclude that their God was a little hard of hearing at best, or a little slow of comprehension at worst. Repetition of the same requests, as though heaven's door had to be hammered down, is a prayer pattern more common to adults than to children.

Nella hadn't yet learned the phrase, "Thy will be done," but she'd learned to trust a good father. She had no doubt that Daddy knew better than she did what was good for her. But did this keep her from asking him for candy before meals or to stay up all night? No. She'd learned it never hurts to ask. Part of the time you get what you ask for. You never know when he'll say "Yes." She also knew that his was a higher will than hers, that when he said "No," he meant it, and there wasn't much chance of getting him to change his mind. Sometimes he explained why it wouldn't be good for her to get what she asked. Other times, she had to be content without an explanation. Even when she didn't know why, she sensed that he could be trusted to do what was right. His refusals were always cushioned with love. Nella was able, therefore, to relate to her heavenly Father.

Nella wanted the weather to be right for that picnic, but she didn't spell out all the reasons why. She just let her request be known to God. "If you want it to rain tomorrow — it's all right then. But I'd rather it didn't."

When she had said, "It's all right then," she had meant it. Having made her request known to God she didn't lie awake and worry that it might rain the next day. She went to sleep. As I looked at her that night, her rich brown hair all over the pillow, her black eyelashes against her olive skin, I saw the peace that comes from confidence in the judgment of a good Father.

You and I have the same Father. He knows what's best for us and will allow us to experience only what is for our eternal good. If we are going to know the peace that passes understanding, it's going to be because we have made our requests known to our Father who knows best.

Don't worry about anything, but in all your prayers ask God for what you need, always asking him with a thankful heart. And God's peace, which is far beyond human understanding, will keep your hearts and minds safe, in Christ Jesus.

Philippians 4:6, 7, TEV

Lord, give me the faith of a little child who has experienced the love and providence and discipline of a good father. Amen.

What Family Life Is All About

The two ladies sitting ahead of me on the city bus were loudly discussing a mongoloid child. "I think," said one, "that they ought to put her in a home."

"I think so too. Their other children — well, you know how kids in high school are. Wouldn't you think they'd be a little ashamed?"

"You can be sure they are. And Doris and Tom won't always be able to stay with her. What's going to happen to her then? You think those kids are going to devote their lives to taking care of her? That wouldn't be fair. And I doubt if they would."

As they gossiped about the heartbreaking problem of

their mutual acquaintance, I thought of the one case I knew where a mongoloid had been born into a family when the parents were in their mid-forties. This mother never discussed her problem with her friends. Among themselves they wondered why. Some of them were ready to tell her what they thought should be done: "I'd tell her that child would forget her in a week if she'd take her away." Others wanted to share understanding and compassion. But the mother chose to cope with her problem without their aid, possibly because she couldn't bear to expose her wounds to well-meaning suggestions and comments which would only cut her more deeply.

Meanwhile, how was her family taking it? The older children, two boys and two girls, adored little Becky. The little girl lived at home until she was seven years old. Then she was taken to a boarding school with an excellent reputation for teaching the almost uneducable. The family stayed in close touch with Becky and she was as happy at her school as she'd ever been at home.

So what was accomplished by keeping her at home rather than "putting her in a home" from birth? Psychologists tell us that a child who has much love in infancy and early childhood is infinitely happier and more educable than one deprived of family life. Yes, I think Becky will be so much better off for having been loved like that in her early years.

I believe her parents have a greater sense of satisfaction for having had her at home until she was school-age. They would gladly have kept her at home, but did what they thought best for her when they took her to a boarding school for special children. They returned home and wept, yet they had no feelings of guilt. They had done everything love prompted them to do for their little girl.

And their other children? They'd been taught what family life is all about. They learned from their parents that they were capable of accepting and loving their flesh and blood no matter what shape it came in. These children saw that no matter how badly they should ever be hurt physically or spiritually, they would never be cast out of their home. When that mother delivered a mongoloid child, she didn't refuse it. That father brought her home with his wife, and they loved and nurtured her tenderly. Together that family shouldered the inconvenience of having a child around who couldn't comprehend things other children understood. She belonged to all of them. They were a unit.

The community also benefited from their demonstration of Christian unity. Their home life stood out as an example.

Gradually, Becky is learning to live without her parents. They know they won't always be around. Should they die before Becky does, they know that she won't mourn.

One day, though, all of us who love the Lord will walk with him. Becky will too. And then she will comprehend her parents' love and his.

Those who win the victory will be clothed like this in white, and I will not remove their names from the book of the living. In the presence of my Father and of his angels I will say openly that they belong to me. Revelation 21:1-4; 3:5

Father, we thank you that you accept us, your spiritually handicapped children, in Christ, and that one day we shall all stand in your presence with great joy. Help us not to judge each other and the handling of another's personal problems. Grant us the wisdom to solve our own to your glory. Amen.

Demonstration

The entire pantomime on human rights lasted less than thirty seconds. No one paused; no one smiled condescendingly; no one was embarrassed. The matter-of-factness and spontaneity of the characters demonstrated equality.

The black bus driver assisted the white blind man into the crowded bus. As the new passenger swayed uncertainly in the aisle, a black matron seated him in her place. Almost simultaneously, a white youth stood up and reached for a strap. Without hesitating, the woman accepted the empty seat and arranged her packages once more on her lap.

The wordless drama was understood by all on board.

Do You Need Help?

"Now, you clean up the whole basement. Pick up all the toys and put everything in place. When you're finished, call me and I'll check it."

My husband came upstairs. David worked diligently for some time and then came up. "I'm all done, daddy."

Clint went down and, as I expected, found that David had "missed a few things." I heard him say, "You forgot to clean up around my workbench. You better try again."

Five minutes later, David shouted, "O. K., Daddy."

Once more his father went to check. "What are you going to do with that can of spilled crayons? Here's a baseball mitt, and you forgot to clean up around mother's washing machine. You must look around before you call me to come and check. Now, you do the best you can before you call again."

The third time my husband checked, items were scattered around on the floor. Not many, just a few here and there. Without criticism, he picked up what remained and gave them to David to put away. In minutes, the basement was tidy.

This is often the way it goes. We give our children jobs to do and even though they work at them willingly, they seldom do things the way we want them done. Young children don't seem able to see all the mess. We give them larger areas to work in than they can cover before they become discouraged. Other times, we give them heavier work than they're able to do to our satisfaction. So we usually lend a hand; we put our hands on the mower and push, and together we get every blade of grass. Or we take a large shovel and rapidly remove the mountains of snow. We don't say, "You go in the house. I'll do it." No, we say, "Here, I'll *help* you." The child still does his assigned task but because of our help he is able to do it well.

The Bible says that the Holy Spirit is our Helper. Try as we will, we can't satisfy God in our own strength. Like the Israelites of old, we fail every time. We're just not strong enough. We aren't even able to see all the pitfalls. But then the Lawgiver becomes the Lawkeeper. He doesn't say, "You can quit. I'll do it." Instead he says, "Here, I'll help you." He doesn't remove the law. No, the law is holy and fair and good. Christ came to keep the law — to fill it full. He has given us his Spirit to live in our hearts to teach and

66

comfort and rebuke us. When he helps us we can please God.

What the law could not do because human nature was weak, God did. He condemned sin in human nature by sending his own Son who came with a nature like man's sinful nature to do away with sin. God did this in order that we who live according to the Spirit, and not according to human nature, might fully obey the righteous demands of the Law.

Romans 8:3, 4, TEV

Father, thank you that Christ kept the law perfectly, making it possible for you to declare us as free from sin as if we had kept the law ourselves. Thank you for the Holy Spirit who is our Helper. Amen.

The Choice

In my devotions, I had come to Mark 5. I wondered again at the story of the man from whom Legion was cast.

This man lived in the tombs. No one could bind him. He broke his chains and ran about the tombs, crying and cutting himself. When this man saw Jesus afar off, he ran and worshiped him and cried with a loud voice, "What have I to do with thee, Jesus, thou Son of the most high God?"

Jesus commanded the unclean spirit to come out of him, asking him his name. He answered, "My name is Legion: for we are many." The devils begged Jesus not to send them out of the country. They asked instead that he send them into the swine, and Jesus granted permission.

"And the unclean spirits went out and entered into the swine: and the herd ran violently down a steep place into the sea and were choked in the sea." All two thousand of them (Mark 5:13).

Why, I wondered, did Jesus allow such destruction of private property? Why didn't he compensate the Gadarenes for their loss? What was he trying to say to them?

As I searched for an answer, my thoughts reviewed my own life rapidly. I thought of the various times I had really encountered Jesus Christ: when a bride of two months, I was left behind in WW II while my husband went to Burma to fly "the hump"; when our nine-month-old baby, Elliot, our first son, was stricken with polio; when our oldest child, Gracie, had rheumatic fever; when our last son, David, had major surgery at the age of seven weeks. Each of these hard experiences had served to bring Christ nearer to me and me nearer to him.

This seems to be true for many people. A writer friend of mine had a nervous breakdown after many years of ease. She is having a long climb back. Yet she claims she never would have known God or learned such total dependence on him if her life had remained easy.

It seems when Christ comes to us with his arms full of blessings, we tend to accept the gifts without accepting the Giver. Then, when he comes again bearing tragedy, we embrace the Giver as well.

With some people this isn't so. When life grows hard, they grow bitter. They quit going to church and their faith becomes barren.

So it must have been in Gadara. Jesus came to the

Gadarenes with a miracle that would catch every eye and ear. On the one side was the healed man, sitting clothed and in his right mind. Over the cliff in the water were the two thousand pigs.

Was Jesus offering himself to the Gadarenes? Perhaps he knew they wouldn't be able to see him until he relieved them of their wealth. He took their pigs and gave them a restored man instead. But they begged him to depart, and he did.

Now the people were truly poor. Besides their economic loss they had rejected Christ. He could have healed *all* their sick and raised their dead. He could have given them salvation for their souls.

There is no indication in Scripture that Jesus returned to Gadara. He still comes to us in varied ways today. Do we see him in our losses as well as in our gains? We still can choose: either we admit him into our lives, or we beg him to depart.

Before I was afflicted I went astray: but now have I kept thy word. Psalm 119:67

Lord, forgive us if we fail to see you in our lives when they're full of blessing. If you must come to us with tragedy, help us to embrace you in it and never to bid you to depart. Amen.

Rescue

Psalm 40 starts this way: "I waited patiently for the Lord and he inclined unto me and heard my cry. He brought me up also out of an horrible pit, out of the miry clay, and set my feet upon a rock, and established my goings. And he hath put a new song in my mouth, even praise unto our God: many shall see it and fear, and shall trust in the Lord."

Note the progression in this Psalm: I waited. He heard. He brought me out. He set my feet on solid ground and pointed me in the right direction. He gave me a new song. Others will see it. They will also trust God.

Get the picture. Here's a man stuck in a pit of such sticky clay that the more he struggles for freedom the worse off he becomes. While he waits for help, he cries to God.

Just what do this pit and the clay represent? It can't be the situation of every sinner who hasn't yet been born into the kingdom of God. The man describes himself as a believer. He's fallen into a situation which he very much desires to be rescued from. For us it may be sin or a sinful appetite or habit. It could be mental depression. Anyone who's been addicted to narcotics or been severely depressed will agree that these are "horrible pits."

While this man is in this pit, great conflict tears him. He says, "Lord, you know I preached right doing in the great congregation. I never refrained my lips when I had an opportunity to testify. I didn't cover up all that you had done for me in your loving kindness, nor did I keep your truth from the church. Now, Lord, don't withhold your tender mercies from me either. I'm so caught in this clay that I can't even look up. O Lord, deliver me; make haste to help me."

The man says he "waited patiently," but his cry has a note of desperation. He says "innumerable evils have compassed me about: mine iniquities have taken hold upon me, so that I am not able to look up; they are more than the hairs of my head: therefore my heart faileth me. Be pleased, O Lord, to deliver me: O Lord, make haste to help me." What a state to be in!

The Lord doesn't always rush to our rescue. We know that it's his will to give us spiritual blessings. When we're in deep distress, we think we should have an immediate answer to our cry for help from God. This man searched his heart for a reason why he should be so bound in his pit, but as is sometimes true with us, he could find no area where he had failed God. He'd been a believer and faithful witness.

He must have concluded that when God's purpose had been fulfilled he would pull him out of the pit, and therefore he could wait with a measure of patience. Yet patience and desperation continued to struggle in his soul. The last verse of the Psalm reveals his continuing conflict: "But I am poor and needy; yet the Lord thinketh upon me: thou art my help and my deliverer: make no tarrying, O my God."

David wrote this Psalm. He had real enemies, especially when Saul was out to get him. But the cry of this Psalm is about enemies that "seek after my soul to destroy it" and "that wish me evil." Such feelings also come to the depressed person and the drug addict. Life in the pit represents only loss.

Whatever your pit, there is help in God. If you will wait on him and cry to him, he will hear. He will pull you out and set you on solid rock. He will give you a place to go and establish your way of getting there. "Many shall see it and fear, and shall trust in the Lord."

Lord, may my suffering help someone. Amen.

First Cavity

David had to have a filling in his tooth. He had visited the dentist the year before. He had ridden in the chair, had his teeth examined, and had had X-rays. But this visit today, he knew, was different. This time he had a cavity he could feel.

We had prepared him as well as one can prepare another for a new experience that involves pain. We admitted it might hurt.

As we walked across Powderhorn Park to the dentist's office, David's face bore an expression of manly determination mixed with dread. His mouth was set with a barely noticeable droop at the corners, his brow slightly knit.

"Timmy says it's gonna hurt."

My hand clasped his a little tighter. "I don't think it's going to hurt much, David. We made the appointment as soon as we could after you got the pain."

His mood appeared to lighten. Letting go of my hand he walked alone along the curb of the sidewalk, touching the delphiniums that reached up to him. Then he ran down a hill ahead of me. He seemed to forget what lay ahead as he romped on the grassy plateau between two hills.

I wished I could let him play. But we had only ten more minutes. "We'd better be going, David."

His grim expression reappeared. His hand again slipped into mine. Together we climbed the steps out of the park.

"I don't really want to go," he said. His voice held no whine, not even an appeal. We both knew it had to be done.

As we got closer, his hand tightened on mine. When we opened the outer door, we smelled antiseptics and anodynes. We climbed the twenty steps to the dentist's office. A grinding noise accompanied by a sound like a vacuum cleaner emanated from there, and David cringed.

The receptionist appeared in the inner doorway. "David, you may be next."

His face set like a flint, David sauntered a bit too casually into the inner office. While he had his filling, I waited, praying. How mature this little fellow was. As I'd walked beside him, and as I saw him manfully wrestling with his fears, I realized that life is like that. True, there are many pleasures along the way to lift our spirits, but there are always difficult experiences to face — some of them, like the first filling, in the realm of the unknown.

As we walked, I had stood in the place of God to my son. Even as I had strengthened him, making it possible for him to meet the unknown as a man, so I recognized One stronger at my side.

Two things make life both possible and beautiful: we are called upon to take only one step at a time, and beside us walks One into whose hand we can slip ours when our courage falters.

Dr. Nelson rewarded David with a metal ring in the shape of a lion's head with glistening inset eyes. On the way home, we stopped at the drugstore and had a malt. We fairly danced across the park. When we paused on a bench to rest, David snuggled against my side. His eyes, full of love, met mine. We'd grown closer in the past two hours, perhaps more on account of the filling than the malt.

And so it is with life and God. He strengthens us in suffering and sustains us with his presence. Life fluctuates between bane and blessing. After travail, the child; after labor, rest; after six days, the Sabbath; after death, eternal life.

But they that wait upon the Lord shall renew their strength; they shall _mount up_ with wings as eagles; they shall _run,_ and not be weary; and they shall _walk,_ and not faint. Isaiah 40:31

Father, help us to wait dependently on you for the strength to walk this route and climb our hills, knowing that one day all our struggles will cease and all our fears be removed by your perfect Love. Amen.

Does God Ever Fail You?

But as for me, my feet were almost gone. So Asaph confessed in Psalm 73.

Have you ever been in that state? Have your feet ever almost gone out from under you? Spiritually? Mine have.

My conflict wasn't caused by envy over the prosperity of the wicked. I have always had enough and have never cared for more. True, it was hard to see my brother suffer and die over a period of months, but my faith assured me that God had a good purpose in this. I had no conflict there. But I had one test of faith that almost made my steps slip.

I would tell you the details of this problem if it involved only me, but it doesn't; the specifics are irrelevant. The fact is that only at that time in my life did I ask, "Is it worth it? What good has it brought me to yield my life to God?" This matter that had cast me into such doubt and conflict I'd committed to God many years ago with true faith. He had promised to do his part if I would do mine. Now he had failed to come through.

Like the psalmist, I too went into the sanctuary of God, but my heart was cold. The promises of God fell on my ears and bounced off. I wasn't cursing God. I was just holding off from him with a "Let him prove himself" attitude.

I began to understand why people stop going to church. They become disillusioned with the church and with God himself. God hasn't "come through." They expected that if they would do thus and so, God would do thus and so. They had taken his promises seriously, as I had. Yet here we were, I as full of doubt as they, even though I never stopped going to church.

I never shared my burden with other church people. How could I tell them that I, a teacher in the church, was doubting God's promises? The psalmist had experienced this too. In verse 15 he says, "If I say, I will speak thus; behold, I should offend against the generation of thy children." I couldn't risk weakening the faith of a fellow church member, or perhaps one of my former students, by allowing my doubt to become

75

known. I had no desire to do that. But I was miserable bearing it alone.

How did I resolve my doubt? I couldn't have done it myself. That became plain to me later. I couldn't have come back by myself any more than I could have come to God by myself in the first place. At the time, I wasn't aware of the Spirit of God moving me to make a decision, but in my coldness, I made a cold decision. I asked, "Whom have I in heaven but thee? and there is none upon earth that I desire beside thee." In the New Testament, Peter answered Christ, "Lord, to whom shall we go? Thou hast the words of eternal life." I realized that if I deserted Christ, I would have nothing left — not even hope. By determination of will I chose once again to believe God's promises.

I had lived in the shadows of doubt and found life desperate. My feet had almost slipped out from under me. So I said to Christ, "Lord, to whom shall I go? Without you I have nothing at all. You have the words of eternal life. You hold out everything my heart wants. I'll take you at your Word and be patient for you to work things out according to your plan."

It was a logical decision brought about by reason, not emotion. I had no better plan for my life. There was really only one place to go and that was back where I'd come from. It was like returning home.

With that decision I felt my feet solidly under me once more. With the psalmist I said, "It is good for me to draw near to God: I have put my trust in the Lord God."

And what about the situation that prompted such turmoil in my soul? It hasn't changed.

Psalm 73

*Lord, you know the condition of our hearts. You know
if we're doubting or trusting today. Give us the courage
to decide to trust and follow you. Amen.*

Dishes

On the top shelf of my built-in buffet stands a set of dishes, "play dishes," of the blue willow pattern. The set consists of service for six, a covered casserole dish, sugar, creamer, and tea pot. Not a piece is missing.

The reason the set is complete is that I got it from my parents when I'd passed the age when children play with dishes. Why did I get it then? I suppose because my mother knew I'd wanted a set of my own for a long time, but they hadn't been able to buy me a gift as expensive as a nice set of dishes.

Those were hard times in the Dakotas. I remember the drought and dust storms. So little grew one year that we were able to harvest the crop without a hired man. Dad and my brother and sister did the field work, while Mom and I did the farm chores. I remember the day one summer when a cloud of grasshoppers appeared between us and the sun. They swept down on our farm like a plague in Exodus. When they left, they'd stripped clean whatever had come up, including the onions in the garden.

I remember one evening when it hailed and I walked out with my parents to see the damage. I shared with them the feelings of loss, even though I was too young to know exactly what it meant. I remember the day they drove our cattle to town to be sold to the Federal Government, as we had no food for them. I stood next to my mother and watched her cry, and today I weep at the thought of it because now I understand.

I remember happy things too. The happiest of all was the birth of my brother when I was eight. I remember the piano in our home, which had been bought in better days and now filled the house with music and singing. I remember the excitement when company "dropped in." When a car turned in at a certain road a half mile away, chances were very good that it would turn in again at our drive. I always hoped it would.

But I don't remember playing with my lovely set of dishes. I recall my disappointment when I finally got them — too late.

Today, from that top shelf in the buffet, they give me more pleasure than they could have if I'd played with them. When I look up there and see the set, intact, I'm reminded of my mother's love. She kept wanting so much to get me that set over several years that, when she finally had a little money, she closed her eyes to the fact that I was too old for play dishes. As a mother myself now, I understand that she had to get me those dishes to satisfy her own deep need — the need to make her children happy.

In those dishes, I see other things my parents taught me without words. I know how hard they tried to pay their debts. My youngest brother, born in 1932, has in his possession a doctor's statement marked "Paid in Full." This is the statement from the doctor who delivered him, and on it are recorded many separate payments over years of time. My parents considered no payment too small to bring the doctor when they went to town, because most of the time they could bring him nothing.

I also know that my parents always had money to give to the Lord. We gave pennies in catechism and nickels in church, but each one of us had a coin to give. As I grew older, after we left the farm, I became aware of a little tithe box. From this my father drew out coins for us to give in church. Ten percent of the cash he earned went into the box on pay day and we lived off the rest. My father never urged us to become tithers. We just absorbed this teaching as we did the teaching that bills are paid, no matter how long it takes or how hard it is.

I wonder if today's youth consider their parents phonies because their parents are just that. No one would have considered my parents phonies.

The little set of blue dishes reminds me of all this. They're intact, along with my memories of parents who gave me rich training in stewardship.

And thou shalt *shew thy son* in that day, saying, This is done because of that which the Lord did unto me when I came forth out of Egypt. Exodus 13:8

Father, we know that nothing we can say as parents will ever influence our children so much as what we show them. Help us to demonstrate daily that we believe what we say. Amen.

About That Mountain

That mountain in your life — how do you pray about it?

Some years ago, I stopped praying that my mountain would be cast into the sea. I've come to feel that if I can climb over that mountain, or get around it, or overlook it, I may find it usable in my life.

Who's to say that it takes greater faith to continue in prayer until the mountain is gone than to persevere until that mountain is accepted?

In her book *Beyond Ourselves,* Catherine Marshall heads one chapter "The Prayer of Relinquishment." Here she cites her experience with tuberculosis. Her tests remained positive for many months in spite of her great faith in praying for healing. When she finally threw herself on God's will and prayed, "I'm beaten, finished, God. You decide what you want for me for the rest of my life," she wasn't aware of any faith whatsoever. But having relinquished her problem to God she sensed a great flowing of power to her. Her recovery began. She considers the prayer of relinquishment the highest form of faith because it confesses that God knows best. Having accepted the mountain, she saw it disappear.

It's possible to make your requests to God in the form of demands, implying that you (not he) know best. In Psalm 106:13-15 we're told that the Israelites lusted exceedingly in the wilderness. They wanted to satisfy their fleshly appetites. They "tempted God" in the desert. Then we read the disturbing sentence, "He gave them their request but sent leanness into their soul."

This sometimes happens to us. Some Christians pray

for wealth and prestige for themselves and devote their working years to achieving it. But for those who haven't prayed right, their wealth holds more trouble than their poverty ever did. Men who have loved their business and the dollar excessively may find in their later years that love has gone out of their lives. Their wealth can never bring back the devotion of wife and children.

You might demand the life of a loved one only to wish later that God had taken him when his heart was tender.

This isn't to say we dare not be specific in our prayers. When our child is dying, do we have to give him up without so much as a "Please, God?" I don't think so. But I do think that our hearts should desire that God will be glorified through an affirmative answer to our prayer.

Once in a group session, opportunities were given for personal testimonies. Gladys Fryhling, wife of the former pastor of First Covenant Church, Minneapolis, told the following experience:

"When I was six years old, I became violently sick one day. Three doctors in consultation said I had spinal meningitis. I remember the violent headache and backache — also that I couldn't focus my eyes. I was hardly aware of anything at all. This went on for several days. I learned later that the family doctor had said that I would almost certainly die. If I lived, he said, I would have serious after-effects — so serious I might be a mere 'vegetable.'

"The night after he had said this, I awoke to the realization that I was better. My headache was gone and the only sensation I had in my back was one of stiffness. As I lay there, alone for the moment, much relieved to be better, I became aware of an unnatural glow in the room. Quite soon my father approached my bed and took my hand. I remember that my eyes focused for the first time in days. He questioned me about how I felt and I told him I was better. He asked me about my back and my head, and I assured him I was better. Then he broke down and wept. We both saw the strange glow in the room.

"Later my father told me that after the doctor had left, and realizing he was losing me, he'd gone to the basement of our house. He and mother had dedicated me to God to use as he saw fit. Now father was trying to reconcile his feelings to the thought that God wanted me so soon. Lifting his arms to heaven, he said, 'God, I give you this girl. I want her to be yours. But please give me the privilege of raising her for you.' He prayed this prayer for several hours and felt he was looking right into the face of God. When he came upstairs, I was well. Later examination showed no after-effects, and I have had none whatsoever to this day. We have always believed that the glow in the room was the glow of the Spirit of God and that I was healed to live a life of service to God."

Her father had dared to pray for her life because he felt God would be glorified by it.

We each practice our faith in our own way. We don't exercise it the same way in every situation. Certainly we may come to God with our requests, but we must be careful not to make demands. We should be patient and condition our minds to the possibility that he may deny our request for our own good and for his glory.

When Christ's personal mountain loomed imminent before him, he asked first for its removal. Then he prayed, "Thy will be done."

If you remain in me, and my words remain in you,

then you will ask anything you wish, and you shall have it. John 15:7, TEV

Father, give us your Spirit in such a rich measure that our wishes will be your wishes for us. Amen.

What I Learned from Bell's Palsy

While a few of us devote hours each week to our church, keeping up the physical property, contributing to the worship service and Sunday school, and serving on committees, a certain percentage of members just come to services and that's all. These people use the church but don't seem to put anything into it. We don't think of them as the "valued members." If no one worked any harder than they did, the church couldn't even pay the fuel bill to keep the building warm.

Apparently the Corinthian church had some members who didn't contribute much to the fellowship either. Some were downright immoral, some were just worldly, and a few were spiritual. I got a lesson from 1 Corinthians 12 the summer I had Bell's Palsy.

For three days, I'd had a dull headache and extreme fatigue. I carried on as usual, working hard in the church as well as at home, but I felt like going to bed. On the fourth day, I had trouble controlling my lips. By evening, my right eye looked very tired, its lid thick and dark. The following morning we discovered that my left eye wasn't blinking at all. Because my left eyelid wasn't functioning, the right eye seemed to be showing stress. My mouth was paralyzed on the left side; when I talked or laughed, my lips moved up high on the right.

By this time I was ready to telephone the doctor.

"Sounds like Bell's Palsy," he said, "an inflammation of the facial nerve. Were you lying under a fan a few nights ago when it turned cold? That's what I thought. You'll have that paralysis of your cheek, mouth, eyelid, and forehead. Massage the nerve from time to time. It should come back by itself in a month or two."

"A month or two! What if I never become normal again?"

"You probably will. 85 percent do without therapy."

For a whole month that eyelid stayed tucked away so tightly it wouldn't even flicker. I could close my eye, but the involuntary muscle used for blinking was paralyzed. My eye burned. I had to use dark glasses and eyedrops. When I went out among gnats and mosquitoes, I had to wear an eye patch, which caused me to lose my sense of direction, distance, and balance. I wouldn't have dared to ride my bike or even walk in heavy traffic. By the time I'd experienced the loss of the blinking facility for one day, I had a new appreciation for my eyelid.

In drawing the parallel between the human body and the church, Paul points out that some members of the church, as of the body, have more important functions than others, but he hastens to teach that "those members of the body, which seem to be more feeble, are necessary." He refers to "uncomely" and "less honorable" parts of the body.

This gave me a new appreciation for church members. Who was I to judge their importance to the church? God's Word says: "Those members of the body, which seem to be more feeble, are *necessary.*"

Necessary for what? He doesn't say. But I've learned that "when one member suffers, all the members suffer with it."

I can even imagine that someday I might discover that for all my busyness in church work the silent Sunday-only members accomplished as much as I did. Only God knows their prayer life and their witness in the world.

Just as my eye would never say to my eyelid, "I have no need of you," I'll never again think, "We could get along without you," about any member of our church fellowship.

1 Corinthians 12

Father, thank you for every member of my church, including those who come only to worship. Grant them spiritual reward for coming. May they be strengthened against temptation; may they find comfort for their sorrows; may they sense the communion of saints in the fellowship of believers. Grant that together we may grow spiritually in Christ. May we go from the church to witness of your love to the world in which we move. Amen.

My Long-haired Son

We had brought our long-haired son with gold-rimmed glasses back to college in time for his nine o'clock class.

As we stood in the lounge of his dorm, we watched workmen who were setting up a beautiful louvered partition. My son was talking, but I could hardly stand to listen to him or look at him.

Why did he have to look like a hippie? Why did he want to imitate that kind? I never believed he was a hippie, but I was offended that he had refused our choice of style for him. He had allowed his hair to grow distastefully long. Only by looking at the workmen and avoiding looking at my son, could I concentrate on what he was saying.

"We decided at the dorm council meeting that we wanted our lounge separated by a partition from the traffic and the stairs, so they chose me to present our request to the man in charge of auxiliary services for the dorms."

I looked at him, intending to look away again, but I was caught by his excitement and pride.

He went on. "At first, we got some buck passing, but we didn't give up. Ours was the only dorm without any kind of partition and we felt we needed one, too. Further, ours is the only dorm without carpeting, but they say there's absolutely no money available for that now. That'll have to wait 'til next year."

"Next year? You intend to serve on that council again?"

"Yes, I do. When you see the results of hard work and perseverance, it gives you a real taste for it." He eyed the partition with satisfaction. "I'm on the judicial board, too, you know. I stand a pretty good chance of being chosen as the representative from our dorm to a convention in Texas in March."

"You really *try* kids at that board, don't you?"

"Yes. For infractions of dorm rules. Of course, major violations and the breaking of civil laws are outside our realm."

I studied this intense, enthusiastic youth. His long hair was shining and clean and combed. The healthy sparkling eyes behind the mod glasses revealed his pride in his achievements.

Suddenly, I felt overwhelmed. *I had wronged my son.* I saw that he had learned the joy of accomplishment through hard work and democratic procedures. He had chosen a way of life much like ours. He was a responsible citizen. He'd already proved his leadership ability to the satisfaction of both his peers and the school administration.

How could I have missed seeing him for the person he really was? How could I have been so blind to the sense and goodness he possessed?

I looked right at my long-haired son, through the gold-rimmed glasses, and into those sparkling brown eyes and I said, "I can't tell you how proud I am of you, son."

Clouds

During her sophomore year in college, Nella was having severe problems. She'd spent Thanksgiving at home, keeping her spiritual struggles a secret until the last few minutes before boarding the plane. Our conversation had turned to faith and prayer, when she turned to me with, "Does God really answer prayer? About half of the time I get what I ask for, and I figure that's about the way it would be if I didn't pray." Tearfully, she told of how she had prayed in faith for a certain thing and had sensed a witness from God that she would have it. Then she had seen that much-desired thing given to another.

How could I explain God's ways? I appealed to her: "Just trust God. He can't let you have everything you ask for. You can't possibly know what's best for you. If you did, you wouldn't need God." With heavy hearts, we put her on the plane and returned home.

For several months, her letters showed her conflict. Then no mention of spiritual things. Later, we learned that she'd stopped praying and even thinking about those problems.

At Easter time, Nella went with her concert choir to the West Coast. In her first letter from there, she mentioned that they rarely saw the mountains because of the mist and rain. "People ask us, 'Isn't Mount Rainier beautiful?' We keep straining our eyes, but we can't see it. Now the kids are laughing about this myth of Mount Rainier. 'Sure, they have a mountain out here. I don't believe it.' "

In a later letter, she wrote: "For some reason, just before we left for tour and during the first few days of tour, I was becoming more and more obsessed with the idea that God was denying an earnest Christian a spiritual gift, the gift of the faith of a child. I decided that since God supposedly would give a good gift, and he wasn't giving it to me, it wasn't even worth praying for the faith to believe in prayer.

"On Tuesday night, our last concert, our director told us, 'Tonight you're not giving a performance. You are going to sing to Deity.'

"Have you ever tried to praise a person you really thought was phony and so ended up being phony yourself? Well, that's what I'd been doing all during the tour. On Tuesday night, when the thought came to me that I was supposed to sing to Deity, I opened my ears and heard myself singing, 'O mighty love, what hast thou done, the father gives his only son?'

"Mom and Dad, the love that I felt envelop me at that moment was so directly an answer to my prayers that I knew — I knew right then — that I could question God all my life, but his mighty love would keep on loving me. He loved me in spite of everything I'd been saying about him. He loved me so much at that instant, all at once, that I realized it had been there the whole time. Tears streamed down my face. Now every song suddenly was true. 'Sing to the Lord a new song, for he hath done wonders.'

"The next morning, we boarded the plane to leave the rainy and cloudy city behind. Our jet took off through the clouds. Suddenly a view burst upon us that most of the natives of that city have never seen. Mount Rainier and the Cascades, close and huge, sparkling — jutting into the blue sky. When I saw Mount Rainier, majestically there all the time, just hidden from us, I started to cry again. The mountain hadn't changed. It had been standing there shimmering over the sky, while on the ground I'd been looking through clouds and saying there was no mountain.

"God takes his own time, but he does answer prayer. I know. He loves me and my faith is stronger because I had to wait."

Father, our hearts are stirred too to a new realization that you are real — that you reign in majesty and beauty over the heavens and the earth — that you are close to us all the time, even when clouds and mist hide your face from us. Help us not to lose sight of the fact of your nearness when clouds come again. Amen.

Confused

"I finally figured that teacher out. Now I think I'll pass that course."

The speaker was my son Elliot and "that course" was a college course required for a degree in secondary education.

He went on, "Whenever I sit in that class, I get so confused. He works on the board, forever drawing charts and diagrams and illustrations. I just don't dig him at all."

"Well," I answered, "what discovery have you made that will help you pass the course?"

"I'm going to quit going to class!"

Seeing that he'd startled me, he explained, "One night, I understood what I was reading in the text perfectly well. The next morning when he started lecturing, I got all confused again. I had the hardest time keeping my mind on what had been so clear to me the night before from the book. I said to myself, 'You gotta quit listening to that guy, man, or you'll lose it all.' "

Elliot left. While he talked, I'd seen a parallel in his experience to Christian experience. The textbook represented God's Word. The instructor (my apologies to teachers everywhere) symbolized Satan. My son represented the Christian, us.

Things can be perfectly clear to us while we're studying the "text." For example, we accept the doctrine of the eternal sonship of Christ until a dedicated cultist comes around with a Bible heavily marked in certain places. We find we can't argue so we search the Scriptures until we have that straightened out again. We know from the Bible that the afflictions of the righteous are many, and that God chastens those he loves. But when tragedy strikes we get confused and ask "Why me?" By returning to the text we find scores of answers that comfort us. Job said that before his great suffering he had heard of God with the ear, "but now," he said, "mine eye seeth thee." Satan has many devices to confuse us about what God says in his Word. We know he causes us to question God's promises. He came to Eve in Eden with "Hath God said . . . ?" right after God had spelled things out. He came to Christ with "If thou be the Son of God . . ." right after the Father's declaration, "This is my Beloved Son."

We know that Satan sends irritants to beat away at us. Paul had his thorn in the flesh described in 2 Corinthians 12:7. Satan quotes Scripture. He draws pictures on our minds of things he'll give us.

Once we become aware of his devices and keep our minds on the text, we'll be on the way to passing the course. We can't "listen to that guy" without the danger of "losing it all."

Lest Satan should get an advantage of us: for we are not ignorant of his devices.

2 Corinthians 2, especially v. 11

Father, receive our grateful thanks that your Word is completely trustworthy and that your Holy Spirit is a teacher we can depend on. Amen.

The Gift of Encouraging Others

The day's mail consisted of bills, circulars, and one letter from a stranger named Don Jennings. He wrote, "For the last twenty years, I've had a custom of writing two letters each Monday morning to the two people who inspired me most the past week." He then went on to thank me for an article of mine which he'd read in the *Writer's Digest.*

In answering his letter, I complimented him on this beautiful thing he was doing. In correspondence with Mr. Jennings, I learned that he was a retired minister who was getting as much inspiration and blessing from this practice as he was giving others.

The Bible lists "encouragement" in the list of gifts given to the church. You won't find it in your King James translation of Romans 12 because there the word is translated "exhort." But newer translations use "encourage" in verse 8. *Good News for Modern Man* reads: "If it is to encourage others, we must do so."

One time as a young mother I taught Daily Vacation Bible School. It was a two-week school, and at the end of the first week I was exhausted. Coming home at noon each day, my own children cross from hunger and frustration, I rushed around getting their lunch and putting the younger ones down for naps. Then all my work would be staring at me, waiting to be done, plus the preparations for the next day's school. I was about to call the director and tell him I couldn't possibly teach another week.

Then I was encouraged by a good friend. Betty, a childless woman who played aunt to my children (and everyone else's), reminded me that in our small church we didn't have many teachers. She pointed out that whoever might start teaching now would start under a handicap. But she didn't leave me feeling so guilty I couldn't quit. She showed me little things I'd done which, she said, showed I was having success with the VBS children.

Betty urged me to feed my own children at noon, take a little rest before going on with my work, and see if I couldn't last out the remaining week. God used her encouragement not only to keep me going, but to do it with joy.

Wouldn't this world be better if all of us started our week by writing two letters to the people who inspired us the most that past week? Wouldn't it be great if we had the gift of encouraging someone in the church who was weary of well-doing?

The gift of encouragement is listed right along with the gift of teaching and the gift of the ministry. It's no small thing.

So we are to use our different gifts in accordance

with the grace that God has given us. If our gift is to preach God's message, we must do it according to the faith that we have. If it is to serve, we must serve. If it is to teach, we must teach. If it is to encourage others, we must do so. Whoever shares what he has with others, must do it generously; whoever has authority, must work hard; whoever shows kindness to others, must do it cheerfully.

Romans 12:6-8

Father, help us to see that the gift of encouragement is necessary in order to make it possible for the preachers and teachers and other servants to carry on with joy. Thank you for this balance you've built into your kingdom. Amen.

No Questions Asked

Nella and Brian were coming home from college for Christmas. Nella's excited letter had said, "They'll all be waiting in the car for me, and we'll leave right after my last exam at three o'clock."

Wheaton (Illinois) was almost four hundred miles from Minneapolis. Weather reports included warnings that patches of ice on the roads were treacherous.

I drew the drapes and put the porch light on at nine o'clock. After slipping a pan of chicken into the oven to bake, I asked Clint, "How about a game of Scrabble?"

"O. K.," he answered as he opened the front drape.

We drew our letters and I put down a word. He marked the score. A car door slammed and Clint got up.

"They couldn't possibly be here yet, could they?" I asked. "I hope they take it easy." We didn't know the boy who was driving the car.

Clint put down his word and wrote down his score. We heard a motor. Car lights appeared. We watched until it went by.

When they finally arrived almost two hours later, my husband hadn't missed the slamming of a single car door, the approach of a single pair of lights, or the sound of a motor. As soon as the car turned in to the curb he shouted, "They're here!"

It's easy for me to understand that the prodigal son wasn't able to slip inside the gates of home without being seen by his father. Jesus didn't mention the young man's mother. (He probably realized that with checking on the pot roast and pies, the mother might miss seeing him approach the house. But his father never would.) I can imagine my husband going out to the main road several times a day, shading his eyes as he looked far into the distance.

I wonder how many years the father in Jesus' story did this. It may have been few or many.

Were we to leave our Father's household for a fling in the "far country," no matter how long we were away, he would be waiting to welcome us back. Like the father in the story, he wouldn't first question us, or scold. He too would accept us back, no questions asked.

"This my son was dead and is alive again; he was lost and is found." That's the important thing.

Luke 15:16-24

Thank you, Lord, that in our earthly fathers we have daily reminders of your love. May prodigal sons and daughters everywhere return to your house and receive your warm welcome. Amen.

Requiem

My brother Jack had lung cancer. I had just spent a week taking care of him, and in saying goodbye I felt it was for the last time. He had had cobalt and cesium, but now it appeared that nothing could be done but wait for the end. Depression and despair came over me. I ached with frustration. Why couldn't they do something? Were we just to sit this thing out and watch him die? He had started out at 190 pounds; now he was 120. His face and neck lay in folds; his eyes seemed enormous in his thin face. His scalp jutted out for lack of padding; his mouth was a thin white line.

I'd visited Jack many times since World War II. Each time, he drove me around to his current building project. On one visit it would be houses — rows of them, blocks of them. "I did the brick work on all of them," he'd say proudly, the "I" meaning himself and his hired crew.

Other times it would be an office building, apartment house, church. "It's a thrill I never get used to," he'd say. "I must have built enough houses to fill a good-sized town."

"And churches and business places to make a complete village," I'd add.

"Yup. It's a satisfying trade. You're a creator. You put up a house and there it stands. It lasts. A lot of my work will stand after I'm gone."

These words spoken in better days returned to me now. My strong brother with the hearty voice, always jovial and kidding, was being whittled away ounce by ounce, and his voice was a whisper.

I knew it would make me cry, but I put Brahms' *Requiem* on the stereo. The record was in German, but I knew the words in English.

"Blessed are they that mourn." The sweet comfort of the Scriptures filled the room. "Now, Lord, what do I wait for? My hope is in Thee. But the righteous souls are in the hand of God."

Jack knows the Lord. All his suffering will be on this side. He is safe in the hand of God now and will be safe right through the valley. Safe in the strong hands of God.

"Nor pain, nor grief shall nigh them come." Only we on this side mourn. In a short time Jack will enter that happy place where neither pain nor grief will come near him again.

"How lovely is thy dwelling place." Comforted, I started my ironing.

Then followed the strains of "Ye now are sorrowful, sorrowful."

"Howbeit, ye shall again behold me and your heart shall be joyful and your joy no man, *no man,* taketh from you." Jesus spoke these words to his disciples. Today it seemed that Jack was speaking them to me. Then Christ came into the room with "Yea, I will comfort you, as one whom his own mother comforteth."

"His own mother." Poor Mom. Old and sick, living eight hundred miles from her first child, she had seen Jack for the last time on earth. How she'd like to put her hand on his forehead and kiss him and take care of him these last weeks. From that distance she has to wait for reports about him. There is nothing more she can do for him herself. But Jesus will do it. He'll do it instead of Mom. And Jesus won't have to stay on this side of the valley as Mom would. He'll go with Jack right through the valley.

I picked up my last shirt. "Here on earth we have no continuing place."

This reminded me of Jack's trade. Yes, his structures would stand after he was gone, but not forever. Here on earth we have no continuing place, howbeit we seek one to come.

The *Requiem* had moved on to "Lo, I unfold unto you a mystery. We shall not all sleep when he cometh. But we shall all be changed. *All be changed.* In a moment, a *moment,* in the twinkling of an eye at the sound of the trumpet."

I stood apart from my iron and listened to the drama building up: "For the trumpet shall sound, and the dead shall be raised incorruptible. And all we shall be changed. Then, what of old was written, the same shall be brought to pass. For death shall be swallowed in victory. Grave, where is thy triumph? Death, O where is thy sting? Thy sting, Death, where is thy sting? Grave, where is thy triumph? Death, where is thy sting?"

I stood trembling. Tears coursed down my cheeks — tears of victory. "Blessed are the dead which die in the Lord. They rest from their labors and their works follow after them."

Rest from his labors? Jack? I wondered. It was much easier to imagine him all through eternity cheerfully building the cities of the New Heavens and the New Earth. For there are many mansions there.

"Blessed are the dead which die in the Lord."

1 Corinthians 15:51-57, especially verse 54.

Lord, help us not to mourn as those who have no hope. Forgive us when we set our minds too much on things on this earth. Give us a taste of the triumph you have in store for all your own. Amen.

Off Limits?

When your daughter starts to read *The Godfather,* you find it rather easy to state clearly why you think she'd be better off not reading it. The same is true of some TV shows, movies, and other entertainment. But other times it's not quite so simple to answer our children's inevitable question, "What's wrong with it?"

Sometimes it's hard to pinpoint exactly what's wrong with something. But since it's equally hard to find exactly what's good about it, we have negative feelings. I suppose the question really is, When does a thing become wrong for me? Is it a matter of how close I can get to sin without openly sinning? Are any matters "off limits" for me that aren't really bad?

The people in the church at Philippi hadn't been Christians long — no longer than some of us. But Paul holds up a goal to them. He prays "that ye may approve things that are excellent." He seems to admit that they may have to tolerate some things that aren't the best; they might even be forced to go along with things that are bad. But they didn't have to give them their approval.

We make choices in every area of our lives. We choose our mate, friends, occupations, political candidates, recreation. Not everything is either good or bad. In some cases we have a third choice: Is it excellent?

And this I pray, that your love may abound yet more and more in knowledge and in all judgment; that ye may approve things that are excellent; that ye may be sincere and without offence till the day of Christ; being filled with the fruits of righteousness, which are by Jesus Christ, unto the glory and praise of God.
Philippians 1:9-11

Father, help us to live above the mediocre, always reaching for the more excellent things in life. Amen.

The Shopping Trip

 One day Mrs. Morrison came to visit me. I hadn't seen her for two years as she had moved her family to a farm. I was happy to see her.

After she was seated, she looked up, her blue eyes gleaming. "Do you remember that time you brought me groceries?"

"Yes."

"Well, I couldn't talk then. Maybe you noticed it."

I had. We were both quite embarrassed, I'd thought. After I'd rung her doorbell, I wondered how

I was going to explain those groceries I had in the car. I said something like, "I found some extra-special buys at the store today so I picked up a few things for you." She said, "Thank you" but I couldn't account for the way her eyes danced.

Mrs. Morrison now continued, "I just couldn't tell you what an angel of mercy you were. Now I can tell you." Pushing a wisp of gray-brown hair back into a French roll, she went on.

"We had finished up our food the night before. The children didn't know this. They got up in the morning expecting breakfast, but even the last milk and bread were gone. I had no money. The night before, I had prayed that God would provide for us in some way.

"Breakfast time came. We still had no food, but was I to think we wouldn't get any? That wouldn't have been faith. I really believed that God would send us some, though I couldn't imagine how. As far as I knew, no one was aware of our situation. It was a Saturday. You may remember."

"Yes, it was a Saturday. Marketing day."

"I let the kids sleep late, but they were getting up so I set the table. The only possible ingredient that I had in the house to give them was water. So I gave them water. Yes, I filled the glasses with water and the kids came in and sat down expecting to be fed. Something made me proceed as if they would be eating as always. We bowed our heads and gave thanks for our food. That's when you rang the doorbell."

By that time *I* couldn't talk. That was why her eyes had danced as they had. God had answered her prayer. I couldn't believe that he had chosen me to be the instrument he used to answer that widow's prayer of faith.

Thinking back, I remembered that for several days

before that Saturday I'd been concerned about the Morrisons. Did I imagine it, or did the children sometimes look a little hungry? Their mouths turned down, not up as my children's did. They looked the way I felt when I was on a diet. I wasn't able to put them out of my mind. By the time shopping day came, I'd determined to buy some extra food. I distinctly remembered that my purchases for them had included a large box of oatmeal.

So God had been nudging me for several days and had finally gotten me out of the house and over to the store. Considering how long it took me to follow that urging, I wondered if there had been other times when I failed to heed his promptings.

If a man is rich and sees his brother in need, but closes his heart against his brother, how can he claim that he has love for God in his heart? My children, our love should not be just words and talk; it must be true love, which shows itself in action.

1 John 3:17, TEV

Father, give me faith like Mrs. Morrison's. She believed you would provide what they lacked. Thank you for letting me be your instrument to honor her faith. Amen.

Thanksgiving Song

"How do you accept a thing like that?"

My sixteen-year-old son's eyes showed the hurt experienced by the young when they feel that God has disappointed them. The father of my son's friend had dropped dead that afternoon as he stepped out of his car. We got the news while getting ready to go to the evening service. It was the Sunday before Thanksgiving.

How could I answer Brian? I didn't doubt my Heavenly Father's goodness. He had proved himself to me so many times that I'd learned he always knows what's best for his own. I no longer questioned God as I once had, but to give my sermon, now, complete with texts, might embitter my son more. I waited and prayed for a reply that might be right.

Haltingly I said, "Brian, when you have a good earthly father like your dad, you have a symbol of the love of a Heavenly Father."

"Yeah?" he asked, his eyes still pained.

"When you're young — when you were little — a child never questions that 'Daddy knows best.' You and I both know of times when Daddy wanted to give you what you thought was best, but he withheld it for your good. Other times, he gave you what you considered harsh treatment in order to help you learn how to live in this life and forever. Yet you were able to accept it. You never held it against him."

He said nothing. I concluded. "Try to think of God that way."

That evening he sat with us in church. The bulletin showed that there would be a solo before the sermon. I didn't recognize the singer's name.

After the offering, I knew which lady was to sing. She was led to the microphone. It seemed far — down steps, across, down more steps. Finally, she stood there and thrust out her hands. The microphone cracked loudly as she seized it. The guide returned to her place in the loft.

The organist began and the blind girl sang in a clear soprano:

> "For the beauty of the earth
> For the glory of the skies,
> For the love which from our birth
> Over and around us lies.
> Lord of all, to Thee we raise
> This our hymn of grateful praise."

While she sang the second verse, I wondered if she'd ever seen the beauty of the hill and vale and tree and flower of which she sang.

She sang the third verse, giving thanks for the joy of human love, brother, sister, parent, child — friends on earth and friends above — for all gentle thoughts and mild.

In her sweet soprano, the blind girl seemed to be saying, "I can be thankful. Can you?"

I looked at Brian. His eyes met mine firmly now. His doubt seemed to have been replaced by quiet faith in a good Father.

I will praise the Lord no matter what happens. I will constantly speak of his glories and grace.

Psalm 34:1, TLB

Father, today I will bless your name regardless of what this day may bring. I believe you are a good

Father and that you know best what is good for me.
Amen.

Christmas Tree

"Move it toward the couch a little more. That's better. Now that bare spot doesn't show so much."

This was the once-a-year stir created by the grand entry of the Christmas tree. A seven-foot Scotch pine now stood in the stereo's place. The displaced stereo looked great under the art masterpiece my husband had made with red board, tiny nails, and gold string. Dad's recliner steadfastly retained its place next to my favorite spot on the couch. Lamps had all been unplugged and stood here and there waiting to be reinstated.

"Guess what? This table won't go through either of the doors," my boys reported.

"It won't?" I hadn't figured on that. "Well, let's see. Why don't we put the telephone on it for a few weeks?" So the telephone became enthroned upon a 90-inch round table with red and gold fringed cloth. The regular telephone table was unceremoniously pushed underneath.

After all the changes had been made and everyone was satisfied, Nella said, "Oh, oh."

"What?" I turned from plugging in a lamp.

"Jesus' picture," she answered.

The head of Christ was somewhere behind the pine tree, an unintended slight.

Of course we hadn't said, "We'll shove Christ into the background." No, it was just the evening's excitement, the planning for the festivities to follow, that made the tree take preeminence.

Isn't this the way it usually happens? Carols, meant to be sung thoughtfully, are made into rounds so that they become entertainment more than worship. With our shopping and baking, we overlook the mid-week Bible study and prayer service in our church. In our excitement to open gifts, we neglect to read the Christmas story. We "owe" so many people presents, who give us presents in return, that the "least" of those who are Christ's have nothing.

I'm afraid this doesn't occur only at Christmas either. By our busyness and indifference we obscure Christ not only in our homes, but in our lives.

For by him were all things created, that are in heaven, and that are in earth, visible and invisible, whether they be thrones, or dominions, or principalities, or powers: all things were created by him and for him: And he is before all things, and by him all things consist. And he is the head of the body, the church: who is the beginning, the firstborn from the dead: *that in all things he might have the preeminence.*
Colossians 1:16-18

Father, we want to put Jesus first in our lives. Help us to set our love on things above, not on things on the earth, so that his face will never be obscured. Amen.

The Day
Doubt Disappeared

Have you ever felt that your sin was so great that God couldn't possibly forgive it? My grandmother did. But God met her doubt in a remarkable way.

Grandma had long ago embraced Christ as her Savior, yet doubt gnawed at her soul and took away her joy. She often asked, "How can I be sure that in the end I'll stand righteous before God?" No theologian could answer her to her satisfaction.

Then one day, Grandma had a heart attack. When she came to, my mother, then a young wife, was standing over her. Grandma seemed to be trying to talk. She winced, and her eyes closed again. After a moment she tried once more. "It was so beautiful!"

"What was so beautiful, Mother?"

She lay as still as if those had been her last words. Then she repeated them, "So beautiful!"

After a few minutes, she opened her eyes and exclaimed in a stronger voice, "Oh, that glory!"

Slowly she spoke, phrase by phrase, pausing for strength, gasping for breath, wincing with pain.

"For a moment — I saw God — as a righteous judge, surrounded by — glory — such as you have never seen."

She paused, struggling against weakness, "Then," her voice broke, "I saw my sins." She wept silently. "I expected surely they — would — prevent me — from entering — that glory. But then, then I looked again — and my sins, *they were completely gone!* They were under the blood of Jesus! The righteous Judge let me come

107

in. Would you believe that? My sins — were covered over."

Grandma lived sixteen years more. At the age of eighty-eight, she entered that glory, her earthly assignment complete. God, who had earlier met her doubt by giving her a glimpse of heaven through a crack in the door, swung wide that door to admit her, a humble sinner, with only one claim to righteousness — the shed blood of Christ.

That's our only claim, too. When we fear that our sins are too great for God to admit us to heaven, isn't it because we're thinking in terms of how "good" or "bad" we've been? Watchman Nee in *The Normal Christian Life* states, "In order . . . to keep going on with God we must know the up-to-date value of the Blood. God keeps short accounts and we are made nigh by the Blood every day, every hour, and every minute. It never loses its efficacy as our ground of access if we will but lay hold upon it. When we enter the Most Holy Place, on what ground dare we enter but by the Blood?"[1]

We ourselves often keep long accounts. We torture ourselves with our failures and defeats and forget that every one of them was in the "package of sin" for which Christ died. So then, let's take everything Christ meant to give us: peace of mind and assurance that our sins will never prevent us from entering heaven.

For Christ Himself died for you: once and for all he died for sins, a good man for bad men, in order to lead you to God. 1 Peter 3:18, TEV

———

[1]*The Normal Christian Life,* Watchman Nee, Christian Literature Crusade, Inc., Pennsylvania Ave., Fort Washington, Pa. (p. 19.)

*Father, my heart is filled with praise when I remember
that Jesus, the sinless one, died for my sins. Help me to
remember it was "once for all" — that no more sacrifice
needs to be made for my sin, and that one day I shall
enter heaven. Amen.*

Patterns

Mother had spent four weeks with my
father in the Bismarck hospital while he
was in and out of the intensive care unit.
Most of that time she slept in a waiting
room near him. Only occasionally did she leave the
hospital to sleep on a bed in a friend's home.

Now he was somewhat better, and Mother felt she
could leave him and go with me to the sleeping room
I'd taken across the street. I promised my father that,
after seeing Mother to bed, I'd return to him for a couple
more hours.

Full of arthritis and greatly fatigued, Mother longed
for bed. With effort, she pulled her pain-wracked
body up the fourteen steps to the room. I unlocked the
door. Mother shuffled to a chair. "I think I'll lock the
door when you go back to the hospital," she said. "I
don't like to be here alone."

Many years earlier, Mother had stayed in this rooming
house for a week when her mother was a patient in
that hospital. Not realizing that such a question might
be misinterpreted, she'd asked a male tenant of an
adjoining room what time it was. Later, when he
knocked several times at her door, she interpreted his
interest as a menace and became terrified. Now, forty
years later, she relived that fear.

"Mom," I said, "if you go to sleep, how will I get in after seeing Dad?"

She sat there on the edge of her bed in her old flannel nightgown. (Her good ones were at home in the cedar chest.) Her face seemed swollen and her eyes dim. She had pinned up her bangs with bobby pins, but the rest of her hair, more brown than gray, hung stiffly about her face. She thought for only a moment. "Say, 'Mama.' "

"You'll hear me?"

"Yah, I'll hear you. Just say, 'Mama.' "

I went back to the hospital. Dad was sleeping. I took the easy chair at the foot of his bed.

"Mama." My own children had used various forms of the word. Only Grace still says "Mama," and something precious happens inside of me every time this full-grown daughter says it. Nella almost always calls me "Mother" and to the three boys I'm "Mom."

Sitting there in that chair that night, I remembered how all the kids would holler for me when they got home from school. (I hadn't been liberated yet then.)

I remembered the times they came to my bed. "I had a bad dream." Recently in a dream of my own, Brian had stood at my bed tearfully saying, "Mama." I heard him so clearly that I woke up and wondered if my college-age son was in trouble.

I had the understanding with all the children, as they grew up and stayed out later at night, that when they got home they'd let me know. That way, should I wake up during the night, I'd be sure they were in. As they passed my door, they'd say, "Mom," and I'd answer, "O. K.," and turn over and go back to sleep.

Dad squirmed on his sick bed. I helped him put his toes out from under the sheet.

110

The children shared the good and the bad with me. Sitting in the hospital I remembered one night when Elliot's excitement had reached me in my sleep. In my dream I'd seen him approaching the house with a happy face and bouncy step. When he saw me at the window, he shouted, "Mom!" That woke me up. It was late. I wondered if he was in trouble. Probably not. He had seemed too happy. An hour later, he came home.

The next morning, I asked him, "What were you doing at 1:20 last night?"

He thought a minute then said, "At 1:20 we were talking about whether we should bowl another game or go home. I'd just scored 142 and that was the highest I'd ever gotten."

"Do you recall thinking anything at all about me at that time?"

"Oh, yeah! I was thinking, 'Wait, 'til I tell Mom this!' "

Dad woke up. "Are you still here? Why don't you go and get some rest?"

"O. K., I'll go now." I kissed him. "Good night, Daddy."

I crossed the street to join the old woman who had long ago mothered the four of us. It was to her bed that we'd gone when we had bad dreams; it was her kisses that had healed our bruises. She had always been proud of our modest "triumphs." When we went on dates, we told her when we got home so she wouldn't worry. For instant response, all we had to say was "Mama."

Softly I climbed the stairs. I paused in front of our sleeping room. "Mama," I whispered.

"Yah?" she replied. Slowly, and I knew painfully, she got up and unlocked the door.

Breakfast Guest

The doorbell! I tumbled out of bed, grabbing a robe which I managed to get around me while hurrying downstairs.

Standing on the porch as though about to leave was a man of medium height and slim build, dressed in clean work clothes, his brown, uncombed hair framing a wind-burned face. I waited a little, afraid. He didn't leave, nor did he ring again. Sliding the bolt into place, I opened the door as many inches as the chain allowed. He spoke in a southern accent. "Lady, I'm wondering if you could give me a little breakfast. I'm out of work and haven't any money. I'd gladly pay you, but I haven't any money."

He kept pacing and turning from me, his eyes meeting mine hardly at all. He examined his fingernails nervously, picking at them. Begging didn't seem to be his trade. I was glad my husband was still at home, even though probably hidden under shaving lather.

Waking up by this time, I mumbled, "Just have a seat on the porch. I'll be making breakfast in a few minutes."

Upstairs I reported, "It's a man who's hungry and has no job. He's sitting on the porch." Half to myself and half to Clint I added, "I don't think he should come in."

(*Lord, when did we see you hungry?*)

More to myself than to my husband I said now, "I wonder if he's cold."

"You better not let him in. We don't know him from Adam."

"I can't forget how he looks. He doesn't look dangerous. He could be anybody's husband or father or son."

"Can't you just take him some food?" Clint suggested.

Feed a man on that cold porch? "Come and meet him, Clint. He's no ordinary bum."

I went down and lit the oven. The heat felt good. I thought of the man sitting out on the porch. How dreadful to be hungry and cold — and alone.

Praying, I returned to the porch, this time going out to speak to him. "Are you cold?"

"Well, not too bad. It's sort of chilly, but I'm lucky. I'm dressed pretty warm," he said, indicating his blue denim jacket, which I suspected was unlined.

"Where did you spend the night?"

"Well, ma'am, I just walked the streets. I came into town yesterday. I'm from Tennessee, and I hitchhiked up here."

(*Foxes have holes, and birds of the air have nests; but the Son of man has nowhere to lay his head.*)

As I studied this "angel unaware," I saw him as one of the least of Christ's brethren. To leave *him* on the porch would be, Christ said, the same as to leave Christ out there.

My husband joined us. "You'd better come into the kitchen where it's warm."

Our visitor appeared grateful. I made hot cakes and coffee. All the while he ate, he chatted. He had no traces of bitterness in his voice and his face had pleasant lines. He ate eight pancakes and drank three cups of coffee. "Last I ate was a doughnut in Iowa yesterday afternoon," he confided.

He also said he had a wife in Tennessee, but no children. "I'd hoped to send her some money today," he said wistfully.

113

As he made ready to go, we gave him bus fare and urged him to check in at the Revival Mission downtown. With wonder in his voice he said, "I'm just a stranger to you, but you've treated me like a member of the family."

Slowly, he moved away from us.

(*I was hungry and you gave me food. I was thirsty and you gave me drink. I was a stranger and you welcomed me. . . . As you did it to one of the least of these my brethren, you did it to me.*)

Thank you, Lord, that we can serve you by serving each other. Amen.

When Were You Born Again?

At our weekly Bible study we got on the subject of the new birth. We had read John 3 and the teacher asked the question, "Does everyone have to be born again?" We all agreed that everyone did. Why? Because Jesus said, "Except a man be born of water and of the Spirit, he cannot enter into the kingdom of God." We agreed that "born of water" referred to physical birth, not baptism, since we didn't feel the Word taught that baptism was a requirement for salvation. Also, Jesus later said, "That which is born of the flesh is flesh and that which is born of the spirit is spirit," contrasting the physical with the spiritual.

Then the question was raised, "Do you have to be able to say exactly *when* you were born again by the

Spirit of God?" Some of the people there said, "No." They considered themselves born again but couldn't point to a specific time it had occurred. Others insisted that if you couldn't give the time and place, you hadn't been born again. It could have occurred when you were little, they said, but you should remember a certain time when this birth into the Kingdom occurred.

One woman doubted if it was necessary to remember it. She insisted that all of her children had given consent to Jesus as their Savior and Lord so early that they might not remember it. She believed their decisions were valid because they were made with the faith of a little child and the Holy Spirit was witness to it. This woman maintained that her own regeneration had occurred so early she had no remembrance of it at all, yet she had never lived anything but a Christian life.

Some of those who believed you had to know day-and-hour of conversion were looking very dubious. One woman, blushing a painful red, told of a person she'd known as a teen-ager who had insisted she was a Christian. Then one night she went forward at an evangelistic meeting and after that she knew she had never really been saved before. I interpreted this woman's discomfort as meaning she was aware she was telling about half of us that we'd never been born again.

Someone else threw out the possibility that regeneration could even occur prior to birth. Hadn't Jesus compared it to the wind? If it couldn't always be seen or felt, wasn't it possible that one could be saved before he was born? She referred us to Jeremiah 1:5 where God says to Jeremiah, "Before I formed thee in the belly I knew thee; and before thou camest forth out of the womb I sanctified thee and I ordained thee a prophet unto the nations."

We thought that over, but the lady most insistent upon the day-and-hour experience tossed that verse out as belonging to a "different dispensation."

Some believed that regeneration could occur at the time of baptism. Others shrank from the thought of baptizing infants.

All this sent me home to rethink the new birth. I was one of those who couldn't remember a day when I wasn't a Christian, though I did remember many experiences from childhood and onward that had solidified my stand for Christ.

My parents had nurtured me in the Word of God from infancy. Three times a day my father read to his family from the King James translation of the Bible and led in prayer. Every night I climbed on his lap and he would tell, not read, a Bible story using a book as a guide, making sure I saw the pictures. My mother talked with us freely about our need for a Savior and testified to us that when she was a young mother she had knelt by a chair in her kitchen and confessed her sins. A great burden had fallen away and great peace had taken its place.

I've never asked my parents if I ever asked Jesus to come into my heart. It seems as though all my life I've said, "Yes" to God. When I was thirteen years old, I went before the board of my church and confessed Christ as my Savior and Lord. I wondered at the time why several of those men had tears in their eyes when they shook hands with me afterward. While my spiritual life had its ups and downs I never doubted I was a Christian. And no amount of arguing that one has to name time and place has ever shaken my certainty.

How can I be so sure?

The Holy Spirit doesn't lie: I have his witness that I'm a child of God. He witnesses to me by giving me

116

this assurance, by guiding me in the study of his Word, by showing me what sin is, and keeping me from sinning. When I do sin, he gives me sincere repentance.

All of this makes me certain that I was "in Christ" when he died and when he rose from the dead. I have been baptized into him. I don't know when or how it happened. I can only judge the evidence that it's happened.

Does this mean that I don't believe everyone has to be born again? It does not.

Christ said that except a man was born both of water and of the Spirit, he couldn't enter the kingdom of God. But he didn't say how or when this might occur. I don't believe that one has to put his hand up and go forward at a meeting in order to be born again, as if the act had to be notarized. I believe that when anyone of any age sees himself as a sinner and acknowledges Christ as his Savior, the Holy Spirit seals that confession forever. And I think it's possible that God still sanctifies some people before they're born.

The question then isn't, "When were you born again?" but "Were you born again?" Each of us has to answer it for himself.

Know ye not that so many of us as were baptized into Jesus Christ were baptized into his death? Therefore, we are buried with him by baptism into death: that like as Christ was raised up from the dead by the glory of the Father, even so we also should walk in newness of life. Romans 6:3, 4

The Spirit itself beareth witness with our spirit that we are the children of God. Romans 8:16

Father, thank you that the Holy Spirit helps us settle the question "Was I with Christ in his death and

117

If the Smiths Hadn't Gone to Texas

 Sometimes we wonder why we go here or there at a certain time. Later we believe we had to be there to do something for God.

So it was with the Smiths. When they planned where to go for their spring vacation, they had no idea that if they didn't go to Texas a young mother would have no Christian to pray with her at a critical time.

Having decided on Texas, the Smiths, anxious to be off, chafed under the delays which kept them from starting out. One of their sons had a concert the evening of the last day of school, and the following morning he had to be in a track meet. What the Smiths didn't know was that if they'd left Minneapolis a day earlier they would have come and gone from a certain campsite in Texas before the hour they were needed there.

They got into Texas and traveled to the Gulf, where they found the campsites filling up rapidly. They found an opening where they expected to stay one night and then move farther south along the shore. The next morning they learned that 60,000 young people would be arriving on the beaches that day, so the Smiths decided to stay where they were for an extra day and do

118

their laundry. In looking back, they see how God was in all of these decisions, lovingly providing a comforter for one of his children.

When the Smiths returned from doing their laundry, they learned that ten-year-old Bobby Brown had been missing from the campground since morning. Many had searched for him in the sand and water, and were giving up. His mother said she felt certain he wouldn't have gone in the water because he was afraid of it. He and several other children had played on a sand hill and none of them remembered seeing him since.

Darkness had fallen when the Smiths and a few others met these parents at the hill to resume the search. The father of the child said he felt he should drive once more along the beach.

When the Smiths were enroute to Texas, Donna had read to her family the book by David Wilkerson, *The Cross and the Switchblade.* As she had read, one thing had been impressed on her mind, the need to put her faith to work by daring to pray for something specific in public.

Now as this young father was about to leave and as this group stood about, Donna said, "Could we pray with you before you leave?" Now Donna isn't a forward person. When there's someone else to say the word or pray the prayer, she's more than willing to let him do it.

This father appeared to think he'd heard wrong. "What?" he asked. Embarrassed, Donna repeated her offer. The mother, already searching in the sand, paused. "Oh, God!" Donna heard her say.

Donna prayed, "Dear God, we thank you that you hear us when we pray. You know where Bobby is. We ask that you will help us find him." Here she paused, searching for the right words. Words came that she hadn't planned to say, "Please keep him safe until we find him."

It was Donna's husband who uncovered the little body. Dale is a calm person. God couldn't have chosen a man more right for the moment.

That night, after the police and ambulance left, Donna went to her trailer, puzzled. She'd felt led to pray. Words had come that she hadn't planned. Now she feared that her prayer may have weakened the faith of this young mother and some of the teen-agers who had searched, including the Smith boys. Donna's family went to bed, but Donna stayed up. She heard a voice calling from outside the trailer. There stood the bereaved young mother, calm though disheveled.

"We're leaving right away," she said. "I wanted to thank you both. Your prayer was answered. God did show us where Bobby was. And he is safe with his Father now."

In a letter the Smiths received two weeks later, Bobby's mother wrote about the moment of finding his body. "I admit terrible shock — but just as strong is the memory of a beautiful, small, grayish statue of my son — not Bobby himself — but a finely carved likeness of him in happy, peaceful repose, as if he had suddenly fallen asleep. This is how I remember the sight — thanks to your forethought. I saw no evidence of the least struggle, or fright, or pain. I turn myself again and again to this memory for consolation.

"In the twelve hours of searching, I'd imagined a multitude of far worse fates he might have suffered. In my heart, I was sure by midafternoon that he was gone, but I pictured molestation, torture, and feared days or weeks of *not knowing,* before some mutilated body would have to be identified.

"I shall long hear your words and feel the love and

consolation in your peaceful tone of voice when you said simply, 'I have him here.'

"I picture Bobby one minute at his happiest mode of play — the next in the presence of a Love so all-satisfying and complete the like of which no one can obtain on this earth! My ever grateful thanks to you and to Mrs. Smith for her vocal prayers that we might know where Bobby was."

We don't know what God may want us to do today. We may cross paths with a person who will never know of God's love unless we show him. We may meet someone for whom no one ever prays, unless we pray. We may travel far to meet this person, or we may meet him right at home.

In the same way, God directs other people to help us when we need it.

And the angel of the Lord spake unto Philip, saying, Arise and go toward the south unto the way that goeth down from Jerusalem unto Gaza which is desert, And he arose and went: and behold a man of Ethiopia . . . who had come to Jerusalem to worship was returning and sitting in his chariot read Esaias the prophet. Then the Spirit said unto Philip, 'Go near and join thyself to this chariot.' " Acts 8:26-29

Lord, when you direct us to go or to speak, may we be willing. Amen.

Look at the Cross

As we rode the new freeway toward downtown for the first time, David excitedly pointed out landmarks that suddenly seemed to appear in the wrong places. Then he was silent. Finally he said, "I don't know where we are."

"If you'll look straight down that way in a few minutes, David, you should see our church," I said. Suddenly I saw it and so did he, blocks away but easily recognized.

Then he said, "It's gone. I don't see it anymore." Then excitedly he said, "But I still see the cross! Look, Mom, see the cross!" His hands on my neck turned my head to the side. "Yessir," he said, "the church is gone, but the cross is still there." As I turned my head forward once more, he insisted urgently, "Keep looking at it, mom, or you'll lose it."

How true that the church may be gone, but not the cross. We tend to look to the church, some of us more than others. We're inclined to place the church over the cross or the Christ for whom that cross stands. Many individuals and churches have "lost" the cross for that reason. The church may disappoint us. The structure, the visible organization, the individual members of the visible church will one day all be gone. But if we focus on the cross where Christ hung for our sins we'll never be disappointed.

You remember the story in Numbers 21. The Israelites had murmured against God for bringing them out of Egypt to "die in the wilderness." They even dared to say that they *loathed* the bread he had miraculously provided in their extremity. "And the Lord

122

sent fiery serpents among the people, and they bit the people; and much people of Israel died."

The people repented and asked Moses to pray to God to take away the serpents which were destroying them. And the Lord said to Moses, "Make thee a fiery serpent, and set it upon a pole: and it shall come to pass, that every one that is bitten, *when he looketh upon it shall live."*

The look saved. They didn't have to cry out. If that had been required, some might not have been delivered. They might have been too sick to speak.

The thief on the cross next to Jesus was saved by a simple "Remember me." No catechism, no dogmas. Just a look at him.

My father had been bedridden for three months. An aged cousin and two of her sons, both ministers, had come to visit him. They offered to sing for him and, as usual, he requested "Abide with Me." They had no hymnbook so they sang a few verses and quit. A look of keen interest came into daddy's face as he lifted a hand and said, " 'Hold Thou the Cross —' Don't forget the cross." So they sang,

> *Hold Thou the cross before my closing*
> *eyes;*
> *Shine through the gloom and point*
> *me to the skies.*
> *Heaven's morning breaks and*
> *earth's vain shadows flee;*
> *In life, in death, O Lord, abide with me.*

A week later the cross shone through the gloom of that sick room and pointed a faithful servant of God to the arms of Jesus.

And as Moses lifted up the serpent in the wilderness, even so must the Son of man be lifted up that who-

soever believeth in him should not perish but have eternal life. For God so loved the world that he gave his only begotten Son that whosoever believeth in him should not perish but have everlasting life.

John 3:14-16

Lord, your cross is very precious to me. Help me to keep my eyes focused on it and all it stands for, because on that cross Jesus died for my sins. Amen.

Stopover in Haran

We turned a corner and started down a familiar country road. Ahead of us, on a motorcycle, were a boy and a girl.

"She's falling off!" I cried. "She's falling off and he doesn't know it!"

We came closer. The girl's head hit the ground. "It's Grace!" I sobbed. "Her foot's caught. Why doesn't he stop?" He dragged her along before our eyes. It was my daughter and her boyfriend.

My sobbing woke me, for it was a nightmare.

For years, I had dreamed frequently that some terrible thing was happening to Grace. In each case, in one way or another, I was losing her. In one dream, we were driving along between two ditches full to overflowing with water. The car door opened and Grace silently slipped out of the car and disappeared under the water.

I was always aware that the dreams in which I lost her physically were only expressions of my deep fear of losing her spiritually. As she had dropped silently into and under the water, I feared she would one day leave our family circle forever spiritually.

From childhood, Grace had shown great sensitivity and spiritual insight. Her Sunday school teachers would take me aside to relate little comments she had made, or knowledge she had shown far beyond her years. But Grace had a strong will and rebellious nature. I knew her will would be an asset as a Christian, when it came under the will of God, but I was afraid it might cause her destruction if she resisted him.

My own failure to help her plagued me with feelings of defeat. There were times when she was in high school that I wanted so much to rest from the daily concern of the teen-ager at war with herself and her world, but even when I was most strongly tempted to give up and let her have her way, God would remind me that he had given us five children, not four. We had to bring them *all* to him.

The world had a strong pull on Grace — much more than it had ever had on me as a teen-ager. I admitted that I did not understand her. I wondered if God had not chosen the wrong mother for this one. I didn't know how to cope.

Then one night, when Grace was a freshman at the university, we had a Scottish preacher in our church who preached on "Haran," rolling his r's. He identified "Harrran" as the stopping-off place where Terah, Abraham's father, had died. Terah never got to the land of promise. Making the application, the speaker named as "Haran" any place where we stop off on our journey to victory in Christ. He warned us that "things die at Harrran. Peace and joy die at Harrran." It stirred me deeply. As the altar call was being made, I looked up and saw Grace down at the front of the church.

125

Grace had taken Christ into her heart as a young child. That night, under the ministry and counseling of a Scottish preacher, she moved on from Haran.

I have never again had a nightmare in which I lost her. God sealed to me that night, and has continued to assure me since, that this one of ours too shall some day successfully complete her journey to the land of promise.